D1497835

PROJECT LEARNING WITH 3D PRINTING

Future Uses and Possibilities of 3D Printing

JERI FREEDMAN

Cavendish
Square

New York

Published in 2018 by Cavendish Square Publishing, LLC
243 5th Avenue, Suite 136, New York, NY 10016

Copyright © 2018 by Cavendish Square Publishing, LLC

First Edition

Website: cavendishsq.com

This publication represents the opinions and views of the author based on his or her personal experience, knowledge, and research. The information in this book serves as a general guide only. The author and publisher have used their best efforts in preparing this book and disclaim liability rising directly or indirectly from the use and application of this book.

All websites were available and accurate when this book was sent to press.

Library of Congress Cataloging-in-Publication Data

Names: Freedman, Jeri.
Title: Future uses and possibilities of 3D printing / Jeri Freedman.
Description: New York : Cavendish Square Publishing, 2018. | Series: Project learning with 3D printing | Includes bibliographical references and index.
Identifiers: LCCN ISBN 9781502634214 (pbk.) | ISBN 9781502631541 (library bound) | ISBN 9781502631558 (ebook)
Subjects: LCSH: Three-dimensional printing--Juvenile literature. | Technological innovations--Juvenile literature.
Classification: LCC TS171.95 F68 2018 | DDC 621.9/88--dc23

Editorial Director: David McNamara
Editor: Fletcher Doyle
Copy Editor: Nathan Heidelberger
Associate Art Director: Amy Greenan
Designer: Alan Sliwinski
Production Coordinator: Karol Szymczuk
Photo Research: J8 Media

Printed in the United States of America

CONTENTS

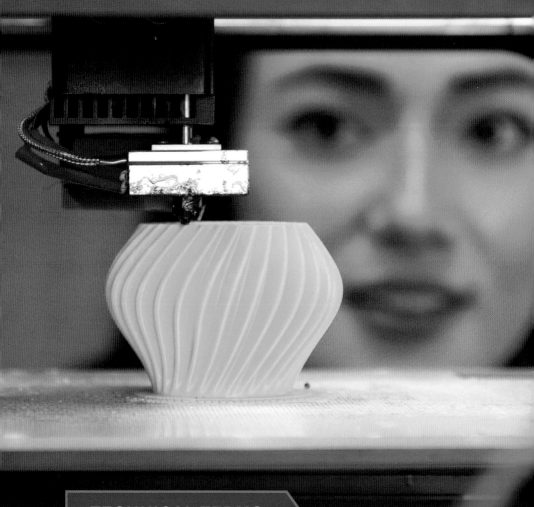

TECHNICAL TERMS

composite A compound composed of two or more materials, such as plastic with glass fibers embedded in it.

computer-aided design (CAD) A process in which a user draws a 2D or 3D design using computer software to create a "digital blueprint" of an object or structure.

stereolithography A 3D printing process that uses a computer-controlled moving laser to solidify a liquid polymer layer by layer to create an object. The polymer hardens when contacted by the laser light.

CHAPTER ONE

What Is 3D Printing?

3D PRINTING CONSISTS OF A VARIETY OF PROCESSES AND technologies that allow the creation of parts and products in a number of different materials, by laying down the material layer after layer until a 3D object is created. Prior to the development of 3D printing, commercial parts, **prototypes**, and unique parts had to be made by casting, molding, or machining. 3D printing is faster and more cost effective. The process is unique in that it builds an object from a digital representation, created on a **computer-aided design (CAD)** system. Because of the technology's digital nature, almost anything a user can imagine can be produced by a 3D printer. At

Opposite: 3D printing makes it possible to produce custom parts with unique geometries.

first, the technology was used primarily in industrial applications, but it is now being used in a wide range of commercial, medical, scientific, and creative applications. New uses of 3D printing are constantly emerging, and this is likely to continue to be the case well into the future.

A Different Type of Manufacturing

3D printing removes many of the financial and physical constraints of traditional manufacturing, which requires tools and dies (forms that cut material into a specific shape). If one wants to make a prototype of a product by traditional methods, one must first make a mold or die, and **fixtures** to hold the parts being manufactured—all of which is expensive—and then construct the parts and assemble them. If changes need to be made to the prototype, the whole assembly must be redone. This process is both costly and time consuming.

3D printing does not require dies, molds, or fixtures. A product is simply built up by an application of material layer by layer. 3D printing speeds up the process of developing new products because it allows a range of variants to be created quickly. It enhances innovation because trying unconventional designs or multiple designs can be done inexpensively. This ability to try variants of a design without vast expense also supports the development of better products.

3D printing is beginning to be recognized as an energy-efficient way to produce parts. The process wastes less material than conventional manufacturing technologies. It also eliminates the need to manufacture dies and molds, which require energy to produce. So, it has a smaller **carbon footprint**. In addition, in some cases recycled plastic can be used as a material, which makes the process environmentally friendly.

Materials commonly used in 3D printing include plastics, metals, ceramics, and sand, with plastic being the most commonly used material. However, research is being done on using other materials, including biomaterials and food, such as sugar and chocolate. The various types of 3D printers employ different technologies that process specific materials in a particular way. Some materials are better suited to a particular application than others. So are some methodologies–powdered materials that are laid down and melted work better for some types of applications, depending on the qualities desired, such as strength, complex form, weight, durability, biocompatibility, and so on. Some 3D printers deposit powdered nylon, plastic, ceramic, or metal and then melt or fuse the powder particles with light/heat into the specified shape. Other printers use thin layers of a **polymer** resin that are fused with a laser. Still another form of 3D printing sprays fine droplets, much the way an inkjet printer sprays ink on paper, and uses a binding agent to bond the layers. Most entry-level printers **extrude**, or push out, plastic **filaments** through a heated extruder, forming layers from which the object is built up.

A 3D printer extrudes a plastic filament, from which the object is formed.

3D printing has the potential to be a disruptive technology, radically altering the product development process. Because of the ease of making prototypes, it can speed up the development of new products and new versions of existing ones. As the price of 3D printers has decreased, it has become possible for small businesses and even individuals to make their ideas for new products a reality. The availability of 3D printing has also spawned new opportunities in businesses that create 3D prototypes and custom parts, and has led to the creation of new businesses in medical and craft applications. The possibilities for new applications are boundless. 3D printing can radically alter the way products are designed and manufactured, and affect economic, social, environmental, and other aspects of society.

A Brief History of 3D Printing

3D technologies only appeared in practical applications in the late 1980s. At that time, they were referred to as "rapid prototyping" (RP) technologies because developers expected them to be used primarily for making prototypes for new products quickly. Since the first machines, the technology has developed to encompass a variety of printing processes and applications.

Stereolithography

The first 3D printer was a **stereolithography** apparatus (SLA) invented by Charles Hull in 1983 and patented in 1986. An earlier patent application had been initiated in Japan in 1980 by Hideo Kodama, but he never completed the filing. Hull founded 3D Systems Corporation to commercialize his 3D printer. The company's first product was the SLA-1 printer, which went on sale in 1987. 3D Systems remains a major company in the field. Like other methods of 3D printing, stereolithography (SL) starts with a digital illustration and uses that data to create a 3D model. Initially, the 3D Systems SLA used a **photopolymer**, a thick liquid that was applied layer after layer to form a 3D object. An **ultraviolet (UV)** laser was used to cure, or harden, the layers, turning the liquid into a solid. The machine was not as precise as later SL equipment, but it allowed complicated parts to be created overnight.

In SL, a photopolymer resin is placed in a vat that contains a movable platform. A 3D design is uploaded to the system and sliced digitally into sections. The machine moves a laser beam over the surface of the resin according to the design data. The laser solidifies the resin where it contacts it. After the first layer is finished, the platform inside the vat moves up or down a small **increment**, raising or lowering the first layer, and the laser traces the next layer onto the new surface. This process is repeated until the object is complete. The platform is then raised and the object removed. After the part is printed, it must be cleaned and cured. To cure the part, it is placed in an oven-like piece of equipment, which bombards it with intense light, hardening the resin. Stereolithography now creates very precise objects with an excellent surface finish. However, the need for postprocessing is a drawback, and the resin that composes the objects can become brittle as the parts age.

Digital Light Processing

Digital light processing (DLP) is used similarly to stereolithography for printing. However, it uses a more conventional light source, such as an arc lamp, instead of a laser. DLP was developed by Larry Hornbeck of Texas Instruments in 1987. It was first used for movie projectors to produce better color but was soon applied to other applications, including 3D printers. DLP printing, like SL, uses a vat of liquid polymer with a platform submerged in it. The polymer is exposed to light from a DLP projector, which casts the image of the entire first layer of the 3D model onto the surface of the liquid polymer. The part of the polymer exposed to the light hardens, the platform moves down slightly, and the next layer is projected onto the new surface of the polymer. The process continues until the 3D model is finished. The remaining liquid is drained from the vat, and the object is removed. DLP can print objects with higher resolution than SL. It is also faster because an entire layer is created all at one time. However, the objects created still require postproduction curing. Among the companies that produce DLP 3D printers are Envision, MiiCraft, and Lunavast.

Selective Laser Sintering

In 1989, another 3D printing process, selective laser sintering (SLS), was developed and patented by Dr. Carl Deckard and his academic adviser, Dr. Joe Beaman, at the University of Texas at Austin. The research that led to the development of the process, which is used to 3D print complex metal parts, was supported by the Defense Advanced Research Projects Agency (DARPA), part of the Department of Defense. SLS is an additive manufacturing (AM) technique, which means that layers are added to build up a product. Also in 1989, other breakthroughs took place that advanced the utility of 3D printing. Objet, a 3D printing systems and materials supplier, developed a 3D printer that could use multiple materials, such as **elastomers** and polymers. Their printer allows users to print a part that incorporates materials with different densities and properties. In Germany, Hans Langer founded a company called EOS GmbH. The company makes laser sintering 3D printers for the 3D printing of metal.

In SLS, a 3D printer uses a laser to sinter, or fuse, powdered material (typically metal). To make a part with SLS, the user first creates a model of the part in a computer-aided design program, then transfers the file to the SLS printer. The SLS printer mathematically slices the CAD design into 2D sections, then uses a laser to pick out the shape of each cross section in a bed of heated plastic or metal powder. (This is the "selective" part of the process.) The laser fuses the particles of powder to form a replica of the cross section. The machine then repeats the process for the next layer, and so on, until the design is completed. SLS has several advantages as a 3D printing technique. It can be used to create metal, not just plastic, parts. It can also be used to create parts with complex shapes, such as hinges. Additionally, because parts are printed from a bed of powder, multiple parts can be printed at the same time. Primary applications for SLS include producing prototypes and complex industrial parts. It is also used to produce industrial parts on demand, especially for applications requiring a small quantity of precision parts. Service companies like RapidPSI use these types of printers to create custom industrial parts and prototypes for companies that don't print their own parts. Deckard and Beaman licensed the process to a startup company called DTM Inc., which was established to design and build the SLS machines. DTM was acquired by 3D Systems in 2001.

The electron beam melting (EBM) 3D printing technique is an additive metal printing technology originally developed by the Swedish company Arcam. The process is similar to the direct metal laser sintering

(DMLS) process, but instead of a laser, the heat source used to melt the deposited layers of metal is an electron beam. (SLS and DMLS are different only in that SLS is the process applied to many materials and DMLS is applied only to metal alloys.) EBM can be used to create parts in a variety of metal alloys, including tungsten, steel, titanium and titanium alloys, nickel copper alloy, and aluminum. EBM is used to make aerospace and automotive parts. With medical-grade metals, EBM makes it possible to build joint implants for use in the human body.

3D Printing in the 1990s

Rapid prototyping continued to be the driver of 3D printer development throughout the 1990s and early 2000s. Indeed, "rapid" was the byword of the period. Specific 3D printing technologies were developed for rapid tooling (RT), rapid casting, and rapid manufacturing (RM) applications. The number of 3D printing companies grew rapidly. As 3D printing became more mainstream, it generated interest among a wider audience, but its applications were still primarily industrial. The 3D printer industry diverged into two distinct segments. On one hand, there were very expensive high-end systems, used for creating complicated parts. On the other hand, more affordable systems were used for concept development and the creation of prototypes. The items produced with these less precise but more cost-effective "concept modelers" were used to explore the feasibility of a new product idea. This area was growing in importance.

3D printing can create complex objects that would be hard to make with conventional manufacturing methods.

Aerospace, jewelry, automotive, and medical companies were a few of the industries that embraced 3D printing for prototyping and product development. However, the machines were still a long way from the inexpensive desktop models seen today.

The materials available for 3D printing have come a long way since the early days of the technology. A wide variety of different material types are now available, supplied in different states (powder, filament, pellets, granules, resin, and others).

In 1992, Scott Crump received patent approval for fused deposition modeling (FDM). Crump cofounded 3D printer company Stratasys Systems. FDM uses **thermoplastics** to make prototypes and production parts. In the FDM process, heated plastic filaments are extruded by the printer to build up an object layer by layer. As with other 3D printing processes, a 3D CAD file is uploaded to the printer, which slices the design into layers. The printer heats the thermoplastic until it is almost liquid, then deposits very fine beads of it in the pattern required for each layer. Sometimes an additional material is required to provide scaffolding to support the soft thermoplastic. The printer has the ability to deposit a removable material to provide support. After the plastic hardens, the removable material is dissolved with detergent and water or broken away, leaving a usable part.

FDM offers a number of advantages. The material is safe to use in an office environment, and the printer is easy to use. Thermoplastics have long been used in conventional manufacturing for molding and extrusion processes. Therefore, their characteristics are well understood. They are tough and can be formed with precision. There are varieties of thermoplastics that can be used to create parts that require translucence, are biocompatible, or meet flammability or fire safety test standards. The technology can be used to create objects with complicated shapes, including holes and cavities. Further, the thermoplastic parts do not break down into toxic components that can harm the environment.

Binder jetting was developed at the Massachusetts Institute of Technology in 1993 and licensed to Z Corporation in 1995. In binder jetting, a binder is sprayed into a bed of powder according to the pattern of the data provided to the printer. The binder fuses the material it contacts so that it becomes solid. Once the first layer is done, the platform holding the solidified powder drops slightly, and rollers smooth the powder surface. Then the jets spray another layer of binder, and the process continues until the part is complete. Binder jetting can be applied to many different materials, including ceramics and food. It also has the advantage of being able to apply color to parts because color can be added to the binder. The drawback to binder jetting is that the objects produced are not as strong or durable as those created by laser sintering.

Material jetting is a process similar to binder jetting. In this case, the objects are built up layer by layer from liquid or molten material sprayed from multiple jets. The most commonly used material for material jetting is a liquid polymer that is cured with UV light as each layer is laid down. Material jetting can be done with multiple materials, and the resulting parts have a smooth surface.

As with most new technologies, 3D printers were very expensive when they first appeared on the market, and as is common, they were large machines designed for industrial applications. The first system that cost less than $10,000 became available from 3D Systems in 2007, but this price was still too expensive to appeal to the mass market. To sell a very large number of 3D printers, it was necessary to get the price down to a number that consumers could afford. The 3D printing landscape was changed by Dr. Adrian Bowyer.

3D PRINTING WITH PAPER

In 2003, Mcor Technologies invented a new 3D printing process, selective deposition lamination (SDL). In SDL, parts are built layer by layer out of ordinary copier paper. A piece of paper is placed on the machine's platform. The printer selectively deposits dots of glue onto a piece of paper so that the glue is thick in the areas that will become the part and light in the areas that are just providing support. This ensures that the areas providing support can be easily removed. Another sheet of paper is placed on the first, and the platform moves up to a heat plate. Pressure is applied to create a bond between the two pieces of paper.

The platform then descends again. A blade traces the outline of the part, cutting the paper. Next, the printer deposits another layer of glue, and the process is repeated until the object if finished. SDL can create colored parts, and the resulting objects are eco-friendly. However, the size of the object is limited to the size of the feed stock, and it cannot create geometries as complicated as those of other methodologies.

Do-It-Yourself 3D Printers

In 2005, Dr. Bowyer, working at the University of Bath in England, founded RepRap, an **open-source** project to create 3D printers that could produce the parts needed to make more of themselves. "Open source" means that the specifications are made available to the public for free. The goal was to advance the concept by creating a community that makes contributions to the technology. In 2009, RepRap released the first "self-replicating printer," called the Darwin. According to RepRap.org, "RepRap is humanity's first general-purpose self-replicating manufacturing machine." The machine is not in fact completely self-replicating, in that it doesn't actually build itself. However, RepRaps do print most of the components required to build a copy of themselves. Other parts, such as belts and motors, must be purchased from general suppliers. Most of a RepRap's parts are made of plastic, and it prints those parts in plastics to create a kit from which users can build other RepRaps. The RepRap website (http://reprap.org) provides detailed information on how to create a RepRap. One example of a RepRap is Snappy, which is an open-source RepRap 3D printer created by RevarBat. It is designed so that its parts snap together and can be assembled in a couple of hours. It requires a few nonprintable parts such as a motor, but those parts are common and available from a number of suppliers.

In 2009, MakerBot Industries, a company whose founders were participants in the RepRap community, started selling DIY kits with which users could create

RepRap printers like this one are an affordable alternative to commercial printers.

their own printers and 3D objects. Subsequently, a variety of other companies began offering affordable 3D deposition printers for sale. The availability of inexpensive entry-level printers has significantly increased interest in 3D printing among the general public and fueled the purchase and use of 3D printers for both small business and hobbyist applications. In 2013, Stratasys bought MakerBot. 3D printers for commercial applications are now available for under $2,500, and units suitable for individuals to use at home can be had for a few hundred dollars. The availability of affordable 3D printers has broadened the number of companies and individuals engaged in the technology. More participation means that new applications are being developed at an ever-increasing rate.

Materials Used in 3D Printing

One area that continues to evolve is the materials that can be used in 3D printing. Entry-level 3D printers often use acrylonitrile butadiene styrene (ABS) plastic, which comes in a variety of colors and can easily be purchased and used in filament form. For users who prefer an ecologically friendly material, PLA is a biodegradable plastic suitable for DLP and SL 3D printers. It is also available in filament form for use in FDM 3D printers. It is not as flexible or durable as ABS, but it comes in a range of colors, including transparent.

Laywood, also called WPC (wood/polymer **composite**), is also frequently used in entry-level 3D printers. It is a composite filament in light cherry color that gives the resulting object a wood-like texture. Nylon, or polyamide, is a durable plastic material frequently used in 3D printing. It is strong and flexible, and is used in powder form for the sintering process and as a filament in the FDM process. Because it is a white material, it lends itself to being mixed with color prior to deposition, or to painting after printing. Polyamide powder can be mixed with aluminum powder to produce alumide, which is commonly used in sintering.

The desire to use more eco-friendly materials is likely to lead to an increased use of plant-based polymers to

Spools of plastic filament are available in a wide range of colors.

make plastic objects. One such compound is polylactic acid (PLA), which is made from corn or beets. Research in currently being done on using algae to create large quantities of PLA.

Metals such as aluminum and cobalt alloys are often used for industrial applications. Stainless steel is as appealing for 3D printing as it is for other types of manufacturing applications. It is strong, doesn't tarnish, and can be plated with other materials to produce a bronze or gold color. One of the strongest metals is titanium. It is employed in both industrial and medical applications. It can be used as a powder with sintering and EBM 3D printers.

People have started to experiment with using ceramic materials with 3D printing. However, their use has not yet been perfected. When ceramic materials are printed, the resulting part must be glazed and fired, as with other types of ceramics. In the future, it is likely that processes will be worked out that glaze and fire the object as part of the 3D printing process. Ceramics are extremely smooth and hard, so their use would be desirable for both industrial and household products.

Experiments are going on to explore various combinations of materials, such as new combinations of metal alloys, combinations of metal and plastic, and ways to apply multiple materials during the same print run. Stratasys's Objet Connex 3D printing platform allows different materials to be combined during the printing process to form new materials. Basic materials can be combined to produce 140 different materials.

Research is also being carried out in using biomaterials (living tissue) in 3D printing. Such materials would be particularly useful in medical applications. Other research in this area is focused on developing foodstuffs–meat being the prime example.

Printing complex parts directly means that the user can avoid manufacturing separate components that have to be assembled into a final part. 3D printing allows the direct creation of very detailed and complex objects. However, there are some drawbacks to 3D printing. It requires a number of preparatory steps, and many parts require additional processing after being printed. For example, they might need to be sanded or painted, or to have support material removed.

3D printing is transforming many industries—everything from manufacturing to health care. The pace of development will only increase in the future as companies and individuals find new applications and figure out ways to work with new materials. 3D printing is speeding up the development of new products. Prototyping is faster than ever before, and custom parts can be made affordably for custom products. 3D printing is fueling the development of new custom manufacturing businesses. 3D printing allows products to be made to suit the specific requirements of each customer. Because 3D printing builds an object layer by layer, it can create complex internal spaces that would be difficult, if not impossible, to produce in a single process by traditional manufacturing methods. One of the most promising applications of the future is the ability to make the parts of the past. Say, for instance, you are restoring an old car, and a part you need is no longer made. All you need to do is download the rendering for the part and upload it to the printer, and you can fix almost anything.

It is now possible for home users to purchase ready-made 3D printers for a few hundred dollars or buy kits and build their own printer. This makes it possible for individuals to experiment with creating products for their own use or sale. Many schools are also using 3D printers to give students the opportunity to make objects or allow teachers to produce objects to enhance the classroom experience. With 3D printing, the applications are unlimited.

TECHNICAL TERMS

continuous liquid interface production (CLIP) A 3D printing process in which a platform is submerged in a vat of resin, and light is used to harden sequential layers of the liquid.

nanometer One billionth of a meter; a human hair is 60,000–80,000 nanometers in width.

photonic The use of radiant light, whose fundamental element is the photon, to harden materials, especially on microscales.

CHAPTER TWO

Future Manufacturing

THE ROOTS OF 3D PRINTING ARE IN RAPID PROTOTYPING because there is a great desire among companies to speed up the development of new products. Most companies have competitors whom they are trying to beat to market with new or better products. 3D printing allows many iterations of a product to be carried out both rapidly and cost effectively. Prototyping is still one of the largest applications of 3D printing.

The processes used in 3D printing change continuously. New processes and new materials will continue to be developed in the future. 3D printing will increasingly impact a variety of industries.

Opposite: These industrial parts for an automobile were 3D printed by an engineer in a factory.

New Manufacturing

The way products are manufactured is being changed by 3D printing. The technology lends itself to experimenting with new combinations of materials. It also provides the opportunity to make parts in a more environmentally friendly fashion. The flexibility afforded by the process encourages new ways of thinking about products. 3D printing also reduces the carbon footprint of manufacturing a product, making it more eco-friendly, which not only helps the planet but also helps the manufacturer.

Most products today are produced by molding or casting, but many could be produced by 3D printing. 3D printing could reduce the length of the supply chain by allowing products to be manufactured at or close to the consumer so that products can be manufactured on demand. The reduction in the number of manufacturing processes required and the number of transportation steps that a product has to pass through reduces the amount of energy required to get the product from raw material to the consumer.

Young people are showing a decided preference for products produced in a way that protects the planet, and 3D printing allows the manufacturer to use the eco-friendly nature of the product as a marketing tool. In addition, the ability to produce products on demand or in small batches reduces the amount of inventory the manufacturer has to store, which reduces costs. Therefore, it's likely that more products will be manufactured this way in the future.

3D printing can help manufacturers with spare parts as well. Instead of having to order and store spare parts, manufacturers could 3D print them either as needed or in small batches, reducing shipping costs and inventory storage expenses. This could have a major effect on the way businesses operate in the future.

Many products today take a particular shape because that shape lends itself to manufacturing by die cutting, molding, or casting. 3D printing allows a much wider range of geometries and a greater complexity of internal spaces. 3D printing is liable to lead to new forms for many existing products and a new level of experimentation that will result in both completely new products and variations on existing ones. 3D printing will fuel innovation. Continuing decreases in the price of 3D printers of industrial quality will also provide small businesses with the ability to create and market new products, encouraging a growth in local manufacturing.

The Aerospace Industry

The aerospace sector was one of the first industries to adopt 3D printing for product development and prototyping. Companies in this industry benefit greatly from the reductions in cost that can be accomplished by using 3D printing rather than conventional manufacturing to produce parts. First, using 3D printing removes the limitations on the shape and complexity of parts that can be produced. It allows the creation of a part with an optimal design that would be too expensive or difficult to manufacture by traditional means. Second, it allows parts to be created with lighter materials, which reduces the weight of vehicles such as aircraft and satellites. The reduction in weight, in turn, reduces the amount of fuel required, which lowers the cost and helps the environment.

General Electric is at the forefront of 3D printing for manufacturing aircraft parts. For example, it has been working to replace heavy nonfunctional parts of its aircraft engines, such as hangers and brackets, with lighter-weight but stronger parts created with 3D printing. It hosted the Printing Design Quest Challenge in 2013, challenging the 3D community to make strong

This aircraft brake flap was created by 3D heavy-duty metal printing. The parts make planes more fuel efficient.

BRINGING 3D PRINTING TO GE

According to financial news website Bloomberg.com, General Electric Co. is betting more than $1 billion that 3D printing is the future of manufacturing technology. 3D printing is the company's future manufacturing technology of choice. In 2016, GE bought two 3D printer companies: the Swedish firm Arcam AB and a Germany company called Concept Laser GmbH. Arcam's 3D printing technology uses electron beams for a fast printing process and can use a wide variety of materials. Arcam uses 3D printing to make parts for the aerospace industry and medical implants. GE plans to expand into new applications outside those industries. Concept Laser is a leader in metal additive manufacturing, and it sells primarily to the aerospace, dental, and medical industries.

According to Jeffrey Immelt, the CEO of GE when the acquisitions were announced, GE's aim is to be the premier digital manufacturing company. One of its goals is to print forty thousand jet engine fuel nozzles by 2020. According to the September 2016 Bloomberg report, GE had already spent $1.5 billion on 3D printing technology since 2010, and the company anticipated saving $3 billion to $5 billion on manufactured parts from 2016 to 2026 by using the technology.

but lighter aircraft engine brackets. The result was a jet engine bracket that was more than 80 percent lighter than a conventionally manufactured bracket.

Boeing's Crew Space Transportation (CST)-100 Starliner is a next-generation spacecraft being developed in collaboration with NASA's Commercial Crew Program. It can carry seven passengers or a combination of crew and cargo, and is designed for missions in **low Earth orbit**, including service missions to the International Space Station. The CST-100 Starliner is designed to be reused up to ten times, with six months for refurbishing between missions. It will have roughly six hundred parts that are made by 3D printers. These

This is an illustration of the CST-100 Starliner (*left*) docking with the International Space Station.

range from **propulsion** system brackets to structures for the air revitalization system, according to news service Reuters. The Starliner is one of the first spacecraft to use production parts that are 3D printed.

The company responsible for making the parts is Oxford Performance Materials. The parts will be made of a plastic that can withstand temperatures from −300 to 300 degrees Fahrenheit (−184 to 149 degrees Celsius). The material used for the parts is as strong as the aluminum usually used, but it weighs much less. The 3D-printed parts will provide a weight savings of approximately 60 percent over parts made with traditional manufacturing technology.

Not only can 3D printing be used to create parts that go to space, it can make parts in space. In 2014, a 3D printer designed to work in space was built in a joint project conducted by NASA and Made in Space, a company pioneering manufacturing in space. The custom-engineered printer is currently on board the International Space Station (ISS). The purpose of the printer is to explore the possibility of manufacturing objects in space. It is designed to withstand a space launch and continue to operate with precision once in space. One obvious future application would be to make required parts or tools as needed without having to wait for a shipment from Earth. Currently, to save crew time, the printer is remotely operated from Earth, but in the future, such printers could be operated by crew members who are in space for long periods. For long-duration spaceflight—such as a mission to another planet, like Mars—the ability to manufacture parts with this type of technology will be critical, since there is no timely way to get replacement parts or tools to the ship. In addition, upon arrival on another planet, 3D printing technology could be used to create large structures for shelter or storage.

The Automotive Industry

Like the aerospace industry, automotive manufacturers were among the first companies to use 3D printing for rapid prototyping. Major automotive companies are still using 3D printing for this purpose, but they have also begun using the technology in their manufacturing processes and are likely to expand the type and number of 3D-printed parts used in manufacturing cars and trucks. Automotive manufacturers are also interested in using 3D printing technology to produce spare and replacement parts for sale.

3D Printing Cars

Automotive companies are increasingly using 3D printing to make **jigs** and fixtures that hold parts during the manufacturing process, as well as using 3D printing to make the parts themselves. The 3D printing of jigs and fixtures can lower costs and speed production. With 3D printing, jigs and fixtures can be made of lighter, less expensive materials, which saves money. In addition, jigs and fixtures can be printed immediately when they are needed, which is much faster than ordering or building them. Therefore, the use of 3D printing to create the tools needed to make car parts is likely to increase in the future, and the process will likely be applied in other areas of manufacturing as well.

3D printing is a natural fit for constructing the cars of the future. Emissions given off by cars accumulate in the atmosphere and contribute to global warming, which in turn leads to destructive climate changes. In response to the need to reduce auto emissions, governments around the world have instituted increasingly stringent requirements for lower emissions and greater mileage per gallon of gas used. If they fail to meet these regulatory requirements, automotive companies will have to pay large fines. One way to meet fuel efficiency requirements is to reduce the weight of vehicles by using parts that are strong but lightweight. 3D printing can be used to make parts that are lighter but still strong. In the future, more parts of cars are likely to be created with 3D printing because of this ability to make lighter components without sacrificing strength. In some cases, the structure of a part created by 3D printing makes it stronger than the conventionally manufactured part it replaces.

Fuel economy is not the only area where 3D printing can help automotive manufacturers comply with government regulations. It can help companies meet higher safety standards as well. Over the last two decades, the requirements for roof rollover strength have increased to four times the weight of the vehicle. Rollover strength is the ability of the roof to withstanding being crushed in the event that a vehicle rolls over. Computer-aided design (CAD) software offers a process called topographical optimization that can be used to design a roof that withstands crushing and meets rollover strength requirements—but the design can't be realized with traditional manufacturing methods. With 3D printing, however, one could manufacture such a roof because 3D printing can handle complex geometries using lightweight materials. 3D printing could also be used to cut down on the number of parts required to create an assembly that goes into a car. For example, instead of separately manufacturing many different components and then assembling them into the interior of a car, 3D printing could be used to create all or a large number of components of the interior as a single unit. The company 3D Systems has demonstrated that 3D printing is practical for creating large, complex components with a selective laser sintering process. Using 3D printing in a way that reduces the number of components would significantly reduce the cost of producing the car.

New high-strength steels, composites, and adhesives have helped automotive manufacturers reduce the weight of vehicles. 3D printing processes that use these new metals and composites are likely to be developed so that more parts can be made of such materials.

Automotive companies are experimenting with completely 3D-printed cars. In 2014, Local Motors created the first 3D-printed car, using an ABS carbon-fiber composite. The company subsequently produced several other models, including a self-driving electric shuttle. In 2016, Honda created its latest version of a vehicle called the Micro Commuter, most of whose body is 3D printed. It is a single-passenger electric car that has a range of about 50 miles (80 kilometers). At the current time, these vehicles are very small, so their application is limited. However, in the future, it is likely that 3D printing will be applied to making panels and bodies for larger and more diverse vehicles. This view is supported by market research. In a recent report, SmarTech Publishing anticipated that 3D printing revenue in the automotive industry will reach $2.3 billion by 2021. One of the limitations of 3D printing for production parts is that the process is slower than conventional manufacturing. However, 3D printing companies are working on new technologies to address this problem. For example, in 2014 Carbon 3D developed a prototype version of a 3D printer that uses a faster process called **continuous liquid interface production (CLIP)**. Soon after, Ford began testing the process.

The CLIP process is similar to digital light processing (DLP). The difference is that the DLP vat container lets only light pass through it, whereas Carbon 3D's vat container lets both light and oxygen travel through the container. This helps in solidifying the parts and

The Strati, the world's first 3D-printed car, was made by Local Motors in 2014.

decreases build times. This approach can print parts twenty-five to one hundred times faster than 3D printing methods currently used in production.

Materials for Printing Cars

One issue that arises when a company is evaluating materials for use in a vehicle is that properties of materials change with the environment in which the vehicle operates. Vehicles are sold in various environments and might have to operate in a number of different environments over the course of their life. Some plastics might not perform well in high-temperature environments, for example. On a sunny day, a vehicle's interior temperature can be as high as 125°F (52°C), which can degrade some plastics.

3D printing companies are experimenting with new composites that use carbon fiber and glass fiber reinforcement to increase the strength of some 3D-printable plastics. While composites and high-strength polymers help increase the temperature at which a material can operate, they often make manufacturing more difficult or take additional energy to process. In addition, blends and composites can make recycling a challenge. Because these composites are difficult to use in high-volume manufacturing, they are not widely used in the automotive industry. However, they are suitable for 3D printing. The auto industry is driving 3D printing companies to develop the means of printing large numbers of components rapidly. Ultimately, the use of 3D printing will grow in the automotive industry, but there are still many challenges to be addressed.

Although most types of 3D printing used in automotive manufacturing use plastics, metal 3D printing could also be used to make parts. David Burns, past CEO of industrial 3D printing company ExOne, has stated that only $1 billion of the more than $90 billion global market for manufacturing technology products currently comes from 3D metal printers. Powder bed and electron beam printing are the primary 3D printing technologies used for metal parts. There is interest among manufacturers in being able to use 3D printing to create large metal components. Such parts are not economical yet, but a great deal of research and development is being

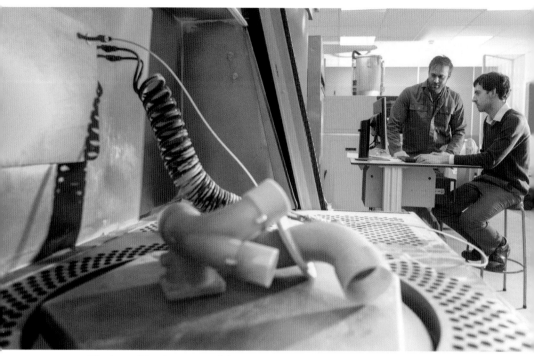

Workers 3D print automobile components in a precision casting factory, a sight likely to become common in the future.

undertaken in this aspect of 3D printing. It is likely that in the future 3D printing processes will be developed that will make the printing of large metal parts feasible, which would certainly increase the use of 3D printing in manufacturing cars. 3D printing company Sciaky uses a wire-feed electron beam additive manufacturing process to print metal parts. Large-scale forged and cast parts can require many months to complete. Electron beam additive manufacturing (EBAM) can make high-quality metal objects up to 19 feet (5.8 meters) in length from titanium, tantalum, and nickel-based alloys. The parts can be made in days instead of months, with very little material waste. The electron beam is used to melt metal wire in a vacuum (a process similar to welding layers of metal in a vacuum). A company called Vader Systems has developed a liquid metal 3D printing process that sprays drops of aluminum to print the layers in a part. According to CEO Scott Vader, the process can deposit aluminum at the rate of 1 pound (0.45 kilograms) per hour, and do so at very low cost. He predicts that in a few years, the process will be able to reach printing rates that are similar to those of traditional manufacturing processes. The company is working on increasing the temperature of the print head to be able to print with metals that melt at higher temperatures, such as steel. The ability to print large parts from aluminum would be a boon to the automotive manufacturing industry because aluminum is lightweight compared to other metals.

Microdevices

One application that is ideally suited to 3D printing is the production of microdevices, objects that are extremely small. Researchers at Harvard and the University of Illinois at Urbana-Champaign have discovered a way to use 3D printing to create lithium-ion batteries that are smaller than a grain of sand. To form the microbatteries, the team used inks with electrical properties to print interlaced stacks of tiny **electrodes**, each of which was less than the width of a human hair. In the future, such microbatteries could be used to make many types of microdevices, such as medical implants and tiny robots. The team has created a variety of inks with different chemical and electrical properties. They can use these inks to 3D print structures with desirable electronic, mechanical, and optical properties. The ink is extruded from the nozzle of a custom-made 3D printer and hardens immediately.

Batteries work by running an electric current between two poles, called the anode and cathode. To create the batteries, the researchers had to create inks with **nanoparticles** of two lithium metal oxide compounds, one for the anode and one for the cathode. An interlaced stack of anodes and cathodes was created by depositing the inks onto the teeth of two gold combs. The scientists then placed the electrodes into a container filled with an **electrolyte** solution, creating a battery.

Researchers found that the microbatteries delivered as much energy as conventional batteries and held their charge for about the same amount of time. Many researchers have been exploring the creation of microdevices, but a stumbling block has been the lack of an adequate power source. The ability to use 3D printing to make microbatteries expands the options for miniaturizing a large range of devices.

Harvard is not alone in advancing the possibilities for microdevices. IBM Research in Zurich, Switzerland, has developed a 3D printer capable of writing microscopic patterns on a soft polymer. These patterns can be

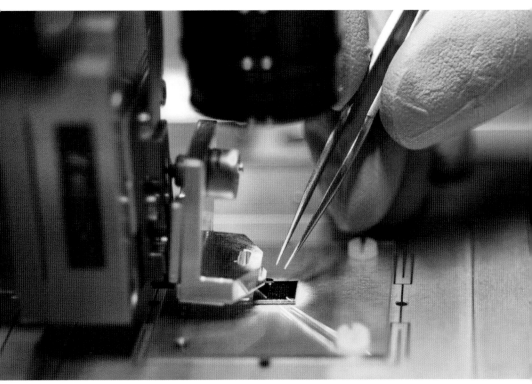

SwissLitho's NanoFrazor 3D printer is capable of printing at nanometer resolution.

transferred onto silicon and other materials used to create computer chips. IBM has licensed the printer to SwissLitho AG, based in Zurich. SwissLitho is marketing the printer as the NanoFrazor. The name derives from the fact that the printer can print **nanometer**-resolution patterns, and from a play on the English word "razor" and the German word *fräse*, or "milling machine." The NanoFrazor is being used by companies to prototype new types of devices. SwissLitho delivered the first NanoFrazor to McGill University's Nanotools Microfab

Lab in Montreal, Canada, which created a 3D map of Canada that measured merely 300 **microns** (about 0.01 inches, or the width of four human hairs laid side by side). McGill is using the NanoFrazor to make prototypes of new nanoscale devices.

IBM is also experimenting with using 3D printing to create patterns to manipulate light on nanoscale chips for **quantum computing** applications. According to IBM, one of the unique properties of the technology it has developed is that it can be used to create 3D patterns that guide light around smooth corners. This ability resolves a problem encountered with microchips manufactured with traditional methods of printing circuits on computer chips. SwissLitho has indicated that companies are interested in using the printer for **photonic** applications such as making microscopic lenses and creating bioscience devices that can separate living cells. Security firms are exploring the use of the NanoFrazor for creating microscopic security tags that can be incorporated into important documents, currency, passports, and works of art so that they cannot be forged.

At the USA Science & Engineering Festival in Washington, DC, in 2014, IBM used 3D printing to create a microscopic copy of a *National Geographic Kids* magazine cover, so small that two thousand would fit on one grain of salt. The process took a mere ten minutes and claimed a Guinness World Record for smallest magazine cover.

Potential Effects on the Global Economy

The use of 3D printing technology has the potential to affect economies worldwide. The current model of economic production relies on the large-scale mass production of goods that are then distributed to consumers at distant locations. 3D manufacturing could affect this model in several ways: localizing production, reducing the need to store vast inventories of components, and reduction in the transportation of goods. A major factor in the growth of ever-larger manufacturing companies is economies of scale, which means that the more of a material or part a company buys, the less per unit it costs. This fact gives large companies the ability to charge less for a product than a small company can because the large company is paying less for the material that goes into the product. This tends to make it impossible for small businesses producing the same product to compete for customers. If they meet the price of the large company, they do not make enough profit to cover their costs. If products could be produced locally on an as-needed basis, using inexpensive materials, this would have two advantages. First, it would make it possible for small businesses to create products in a cost-effective manner for local customers, thus allowing them to operate profitably. Second, it would reduce the need to transport large amounts of products from the manufacturing site to distant stores where they are sold. This would reduce the cost to consumers by reducing the transportation cost built into the product's price. It would also help small businesses survive by increasing their sales while helping the planet by reducing the use of carbon emission–producing vehicles.

The widespread use of 3D printing could create a range of new professions for individuals and small businesses, much as other technology products, such as computers, have done. There would be a need for people to manufacture the printers, both large printers for industrial and commercial use and small ones for small business and home use. More than that, however, would be the need for small businesses that service the printers and instruct people on how to use them, as well as designers who create designs for products that can be 3D printed and sell the ready-made designs to individuals and companies. On the industrial and commercial side, printer operators would be in demand. New materials will be continuously developed. This will create a need for researchers in this area, as well as companies that sell the materials to businesses and consumers. We are also likely to see the "copy shop" phenomenon. There are already a few large companies making components for industries on a contract basis. When a company needs a part, it contracts with the 3D printing company to manufacture it. As 3D printing becomes mainstream, there is likely to be an increase in the number of companies doing 3D printing for industrial applications.

In addition, smaller 3D printing companies are likely to start popping up, offering standard and custom products directly to consumers, much the way that print and copy shops offer their services. These might include the ability to bring in or create on-site a design that the shop prints, as well as a catalog of products the customer can have printed.

3D printing is likely to be a disruptive technology in that it will change the way that many products are made. The result will be a reduced need for some present jobs and the creation of new ones. It could make it easier for people to make products to sell locally, but it could also eliminate the need to hire large numbers of people in countries where wages are low, which could negatively affect their economies. Therefore, it is likely that the developed world would see the most benefit from 3D printing becoming a mainstream technology. However, it could revitalize stagnant economies by fueling the creation of small businesses headed by individuals with an idea for a product and the ability to produce it because, with 3D printing, the startup cost of doing so would be minimal. Much as an individual can create and sell an app today for use on a computer or mobile device, anyone who can conceive of an idea will be able to create and sell it. It is likely that the use of 3D printing to produce goods would have a less dramatic effect on developed nations than on developing nations. For one thing, most large-scale manufacturing in industrialized nations relies heavily on automation, so even a cutback in mass manufacturing would result in fewer lost jobs than in an economy that relies on manual labor. Second, with an aging population, more people will be leaving the workforce over the next four decades. Some of these people will be looking for a means to make money part-time, and 3D printing can provide them with a tool to do so, while their retirement from the full-time workforce provides openings for new workers.

3D printing can become an educational tool. Obtaining adequate teaching materials for students is often difficult. School budgets are limited, and teachers often have to buy their own supplies. This makes it difficult to provide students with expensive objects such as models to study. 3D printing could change that. Some schools already have 3D printers. Science and math are often suggested as applications for 3D printers in schools. Teachers could make a model of a molecule, for example, to illustrate how it is made up of atoms, or create a model of DNA to show its structure. However, 3D printing could be used in other subjects, too. In a history class, for example, it could be used to convey more effectively than with a two-dimensional picture what objects or structures from different periods were like. 3D printers would also be of great use in vocational and technical high schools. They would allow teachers to print out replicas of complex objects for illustration and practice at a low cost.

The commercialization of 3D printing will be supported by organizations that create standards for products, such as ASTM International, which is in the process of writing standards for some 3D printing processes. Having standards means there is consistency in the construction of parts regardless of who makes them. Standards make it easier for a technology to spread. ASTM has already created an international standard for directed energy deposition. ASTM has a committee dedicated to the development of standards for 3D printing: Committee F42 on Additive Manufacturing Technologies. The committee creates standards that cover the setup, application, documentation, and other aspects of 3D printing processes.

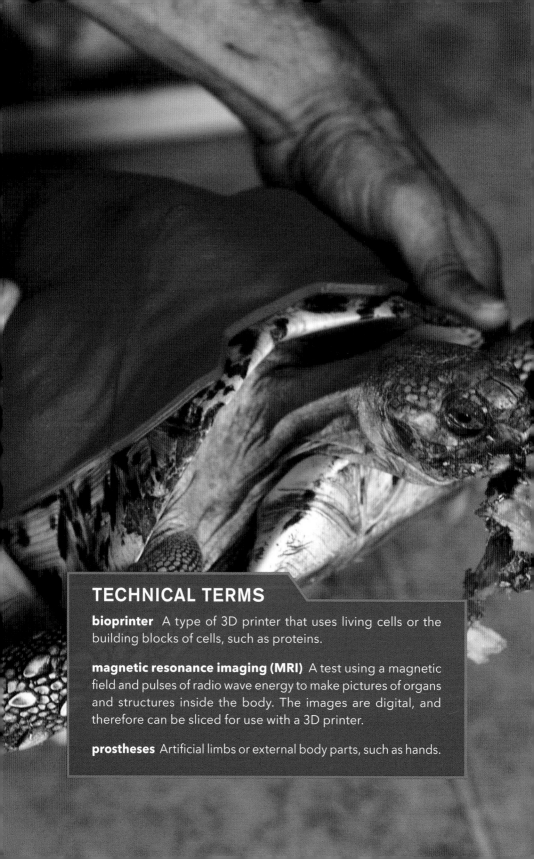

TECHNICAL TERMS

bioprinter A type of 3D printer that uses living cells or the building blocks of cells, such as proteins.

magnetic resonance imaging (MRI) A test using a magnetic field and pulses of radio wave energy to make pictures of organs and structures inside the body. The images are digital, and therefore can be sliced for use with a 3D printer.

prostheses Artificial limbs or external body parts, such as hands.

CHAPTER THREE

3D Medicine

THE MEDICAL INDUSTRY IS A HUGE AREA FOR THE APPLICATION of 3D printing technology. The customization and miniaturization capabilities of 3D printing make it an appealing tool for medical and biological procedures. 3D printing has applications in several different categories of health care: prosthetics, or artificial limbs; medical devices, especially those that are implanted in the body; and organ and tissue transplants.

Organs on Demand

Organ transplantation saves lives. However, one of the major problems with transplanting organs is that

Opposite: 3D printing was used to make a prosthetic shell for this injured leopard tortoise.

the recipient's immune system cells will attack the donated organ because the immune system responds to the foreign cells as if they were invading cells, such as bacteria or viruses. Patients who receive organ transplants have to take medications that suppress their immune system in order to protect the transplanted organ, but this makes them susceptible to infection. One potential solution to this problem is to grow a new organ using the patient's own cells. Researchers have experimented with growing an organ from a patient's cells by applying the cells to a biodegradable frame. The first successful organ transplants with organs grown from patients' own cells occurred between 1999 and 2001, when researchers at the Wake Forest Institute for Regenerative Medicine in Winston-Salem, North Carolina, accomplished urinary bladder transplants, first in animals and then in seven young patients. Tengion, a biotech company based near Philadelphia, has also successfully grown complete bladders from patients' cells and successfully transplanted them into patients who were enrolled in clinical trials. Although few complete organ transplants have been done with lab-grown organs, a wide variety of partial organ transplants have been carried out successfully, including skin grafts, a graft for a patient's **trachea**, and cartilage for use in a patient's knee. The successful growing of organs from patients' cells raises the possibility of developing other means of engineering organs, including using 3D printing to layer cells.

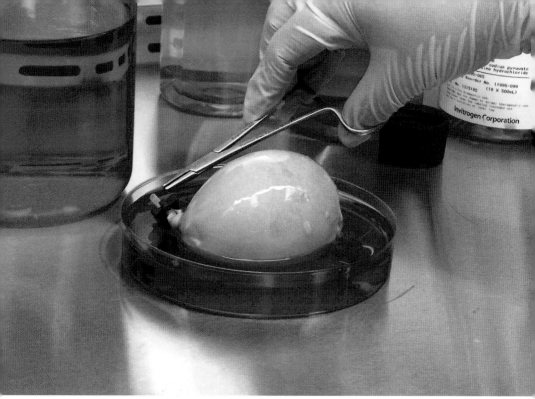

A doctor at Wake Forest University dips a biodegradable bladder-shaped mold into a solution containing a patient's bladder cells.

The Wake Forest Institute is currently conducting research in this area. A research group uses custom-built **bioprinters**, which work much like standard 3D printers. The object to be printed is modeled in software or scanned into a computer file, which is uploaded to the printer. Syringes lay down layers of matter until a three-dimensional object is formed. The difference is that instead of plastic or metal, the bioprinters use living cells. The bioprinters contain six syringes, one of which is used to lay down a biodegradable plastic that forms a scaffold in the shape of an organ or body part, such as a tendon or ear; the other five syringes lay down a gel containing human cells with nutrients to nourish them. The completed structure is then placed in an incubator, and the cells multiply until the organ or body part is complete. Theoretically, it could then be implanted into a patient. Wake Forest staffers have implanted a number of bioprinted materials, including skin, ears, bone, and muscle, into laboratory animals, and these have integrated successfully with the surrounding tissue. Researchers at Princeton University in New Jersey and Johns Hopkins University in Baltimore, Maryland, have bioprinted a prototype outer ear on an ear-shaped scaffold. It combines living cells in a hydrogel and silver nanoparticles that act as an antenna to pick up sound once the ear cartilage has finished growing.

Another bioprinting project at the Wake Forest Institute is the creation of a skin-cell printer, which would print different types of living skin cells right onto a patient. The concept is to scan a patient's skin wound and then grow replacement cells in a gel and print them out in the exact shape of the wound. Researchers have already succeeded in having the printer lay down the top two layers of skin, which is sufficient to treat most burns, and they have repaired skin wounds in pigs using the technology. Their goal is to be able to print the lower layers of skin as well, including fat tissue and hair follicles. Wake Forest hopes to begin clinical trials of the printed skin process within the next several years. The bioprinting firm Organovo, located in San Diego, California, partnered with Invetech to create the first commercial bioprinter. The company also prints tissue

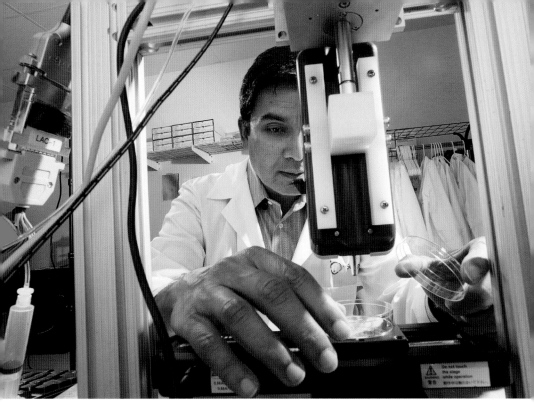

A researcher works with a bioprinter to print cellular matter to repair cartilage.

and sells it to researchers for use in testing whether new drugs being developed are toxic to liver or kidney tissue. According to Keith Murphy, Organovo's former chief executive officer, the company ultimately wants to provide printed liver tissue patches for doctors to use to repair damaged livers.

In cases where it is not feasible to use a patient's own cells, perhaps because of disease, it would be possible to build organs from cells of a donor with compatible tissue. This could increase the availability of organs for patients on waiting lists for an organ that closely matches their tissue, which is a serious problem. There is still a long way to go before it will be possible to build large organs

with complicated blood vessels and other structures—
such as kidneys and livers—although researchers are
working on the problem.

Medical Implants

While some scientists are working on methods to
bioprint tissues and organs, other researchers are using
the 3D printing methods developed for bioprinting to
create silicone implants, such as tubes for draining
body fluids, **catheters** to drain urine, and **stents** to keep
airways open. Silicone is a soft plastic, unlike the rigid
plastics used to make industrial 3D parts. Because it
is soft, it is impossible to get it to hold its shape when
deposited by a 3D printer. However, in 2015, researchers
at the University of Florida developed a new method
for 3D printing soft materials by injecting them into
a granular gel like that used to make hand-sanitizing
products. The gel supports the silicone as it is deposited.
In 2017, the group created an improved oil-based gel
that allows the fabrication of higher-precision, more
durable silicone implants. Using the new gel, they have
made 3D scaffolds; networks of hollow vessels, which
are necessary to create complex organs; a model of a
tracheal implant; and a working fluid pump. Being able
to 3D print silicone devices could make customized
implants faster to produce and less expensive.

3D printing technology has already been used to
manufacture commonly used medical implants, including

knee, hip, and shoulder implants made of titanium or a titanium alloy. The key to a successful implant is achieving a surface that encourages the **adhesion** and growth of surrounding cells into the surface of the implant, which can be achieved with 3D printing. 3D printing of metal implants uses biocompatible titanium or titanium alloy powder to build the layers. The implants are printed in a tightly controlled atmosphere, using nonreactive gases and restricting the presence of oxygen to achieve a high purity of the material in the printed parts.

The Swedish firm OssDsign AB has received clearance from the Food and Drug Administration (FDA) to offer 3D-printed **cranial** and facial reconstruction implants to the US from Sweden, and Connecticut-based Oxford Performance Materials (OPM) has received FDA approval to sell its 3D-printed polymer cranial implants, which are used to repair defects in the skull. Oxford Performance Materials has developed a bonelike biocompatible material, PEKK. Prior to 2006, the firm sold the material to companies making implants as a replacement for the traditional steel and titanium. In 2006, OPM began printing its own implants made of PEKK, including the FDA-approved cranial device. **Computed tomography (CT)** and **magnetic resonance imaging (MRI)** scans are used by both companies to determine the dimensions needed. OssDsign's implants consist of layers of a calcium phosphate composite material applied to a strong titanium scaffold. OPM uses selective laser sintering (SLS) to fuse the deposited PEKK polymer. Traditionally, bone from the patient's body or metal has been used to repair cranial defects. However, the 3D-printed implants offer two advantages. First, they are less prone to infection, and second, the 3D-printed implant can be customized for each patient to exactly fit the defect.

In the future, the use of 3D printing for custom medical implants will inevitably grow. In 2011, a 3D-printed lower jaw was custom-made and implanted into an eighty-three-year-old woman who was considered a poor risk for traditional reconstructive surgery due to her age. The process was researched at the Biomedical Research Institute at Hasselt University in Belgium, and the implant was created by LayerWise, also in Belgium. Surgery to attach it was done in the Netherlands. The implant was 3D printed from titanium powder fused by a laser, and the implant took merely a few hours to print. The creation and insertion of the implant are important because it is a complex part that includes articulated joints, cavities to encourage muscles to attach to it, and grooves to guide the regrowth of nerves and veins. In the future, the use of such custom implants is likely to grow significantly. Custom-made rather than stock implants provide a more precise fit, which reduces recovery time, and the 3D printing process can create implants with more porous titanium surfaces, encouraging better growth of the surrounding bone into the implant. This in turn results in better fixation and increases the amount of time an implant stays in place before having to be replaced. In 2012, researchers at Washington State University used 3D printing to create ceramic scaffolds that could be used to encourage the growth of new bone tissue in implants. Experiments with animals were sufficiently promising for the group to predict that the method could eventually be used for human implants.

3D-Printed Hearing Aids

3D printing can also create external medical devices that must be custom-fit, such as hearing aids. Prior to the application of 3D printing to making customized hearing aids, the process required about nine steps, and even when molds to cast the hearing aid were made from impressions taken of the patient's ear, there were often problems with the fit of the finished product. Not only does the use of 3D printing cut the fabrication time from about a week to a single day, but a much better fit can be achieved. Instead of taking a physical impression of a patient's ear, an audiologist uses a 3D scanner, which creates about 100,000 to 150,000 points of reference. The shell of the hearing aid is 3D printed from resin, and then the electronics are added. 3D printing is rapidly becoming the method of choice for making hearing aids. This type of approach is likely to be applied to a wide range of medical devices in the future. The technology has the potential to bring down the cost of hearing aids–

which currently cost several thousand dollars—because it reduces the manufacturing time and the number of people involved in the process, and allows the creation of more units in a short time. However, it remains to be seen if the manufacturers of hearing aids will pass such cost savings along to patients.

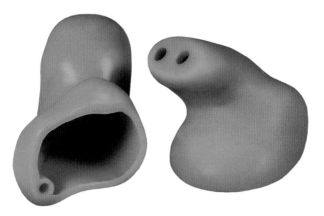

3D-printed hearing aids provide a more precise fit and shorter manufacturing time.

Orthotics

Orthotic devices are external supports such as braces and shoe inserts that are used to adjust abnormalities in peoples' gait or posture, often after a stroke or injury. Currently, the process of creating custom orthotic devices requires considerable time and labor. However, researchers at the University of Michigan (U-M) are developing a 3D printing system that can create customized orthotic and prosthetic devices in less than a day.

The most common way of creating assistive devices is to wrap fiberglass tape around a patient's limb to make a mold. Plaster is then poured into the mold to create a model, and hot plastic is then pressed around the model to form a supportive device. Then straps and other required components are added. Patients must wait from days to weeks for the finished product.

The U-M researchers use 3D printing to achieve a faster and more accurate result. They first take an optical scan of the body part to be supported, such as an ankle that requires a foot brace. The data is uploaded to software that allows an orthotist to create a design for the device, and the file is uploaded to a 3D printer, which can print the orthotic device in a few hours. Researchers at U-M believe that patients could eventually visit an orthotist in the morning for a scan of their limb and have their orthotic device printed and ready by the same afternoon. Aside from the rapidity with which orthotic devices can be created, using an optical scan and 3D printing would result in a more precisely fitting and a lighter-weight device, which would make its use easier and more comfortable. A 3D-printed orthotic device is lighter because the process uses a structure that consists of tiny crisscrossing struts inside the device, rather than the solid plastic of conventional orthotic devices. Because the file with the patient's model can be saved like any other computer file, it would also be simple to print out a replacement device or make a small adjustment to the model at a later time if needed and print another device for the patient.

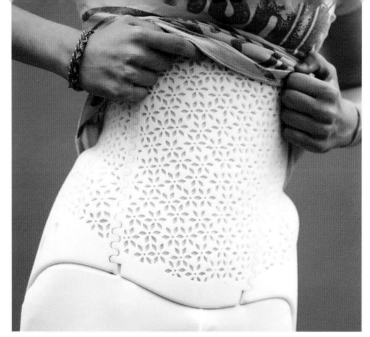

The open-pattern structure of this 3D-printed, custom-made back brace makes it lighter to wear.

Here is an example of how a 3D print can help a patient. A 3D-printed cortex exoskeletal cast is a light, washable, breathable, and recyclable alternative to the traditional plaster cast. Not only is it more easily wearable and hygienic than its predecessor, it is based on an X-ray and 3D scan of the patient's fracture and modeled accordingly.

Prosthetics

Although people in all nations need **prostheses**, there is an especially strong demand in developing nations because of a lack of prosthetists to make them. The World Health Organization estimates that there is a shortage of forty thousand prosthetists throughout poorer nations. When these nations are war zones, the problem is particularly acute because of the need for artificial limbs for injured combatants. Clearly, 3D printing would be a boon to those in developing nations.

3D printing of prostheses also addresses the problem of providing prostheses for children. Growing children rapidly outgrow their prostheses, which have to be replaced at least every couple of years. Because the 3D printing process is a less expensive way to make prostheses, this method helps ease the parents' financial burden as a child grows. In addition, children are less embarrassed about wearing 3D-printed prosthetic limbs that show, such as artificial hands, because instead of a heavy, awkward device attached to the arm with straps, the 3D-printed hands can be made of plastic in an array of cool colors.

In response to the need for prosthetic hands in underserved populations, Jorge Zuniga, a research scientist in the biomechanics research department at the University of Nebraska, Omaha, initiated a project called Cyborg Beast. Supported by NASA, Git-R-Done Foundation, Boa Technology, and Innovative Prosthetics and Orthotics, Cyborg Beast has created a program that allows those in need to create customized, low-cost prosthetic and orthotic devices. The project also provides technical support to educational and medical institutions that want to offer low-cost 3D-printed prostheses. Cyborg Beast's long-term goal is to create "a line of visually appealing, easy to assemble, low-cost 3D-printed prosthetic and orthotic devices for children with upper and lower limb differences." They want to make it

A child tries out her new 3D-printed prosthetic hand, made using an open-source design.

possible for growing children to develop normal motor skills by allowing them to participate in recreational activities and sports like other children.

Currently, Cyborg Beast works mostly with hands, but it is investigating other applications as well. The group 3D printed a complete arm for a child who was missing a shoulder. Not only did the prosthesis assist him in daily life, but it also improved his posture and balance. According to Zuniga, more than five hundred Cyborg Beasts are in use around the world. The design itself has been downloaded over forty-eight thousand times. Zuniga runs a pediatric **orthopedic** 3D printing laboratory in his native Chile and has used the design there as well.

An issue that remains to be addressed is that some of the materials used in the Cyborg Beast can melt in locales with very high temperatures. This means it may not work well in some nations that need it most, such as developing countries in Africa. However, it is probable that more temperature-resistant materials will be developed in the future. The project is just in its early phase, and it holds a great deal of promise for use in developing nations in the future.

One effort to help amputees in Africa through 3D printing was called Project Daniel. It was named after twelve-year-old Daniel Omar, who lost both arms during a bombing attack in Sudan's Nuba Mountains. An American, Tom Catena, was the only permanent doctor for the half a million people relying on his Mother of Mercy Hospital. According to Catena, there are many arm amputees as a result of the civil war in Sudan and the general lack of medical care. Philanthropist Mick Ebeling heard about Catena's work and brought 3D printers to Sudan to make prosthetic arms. In an agricultural society, like that in Sudan, almost everyone must grow their own food, so missing an arm makes a person totally dependent on his or her family. In addition, amputees struggle to find someone willing to marry them, which is socially important in Sudan. Catena said the 3D-printed prostheses were good, but the Sudanese found them cumbersome and stopped wearing them. "Perhaps with some tweaking, the 3D printers can be of great use for arm amputees," Catena told the *Guardian* in 2017.

An even bigger problem in developing nations is the loss of a leg, which results in loss of mobility. Wheelchairs are unaffordable for many people and, in any case, are hard to use on unpaved roads and muddy streets. Without a prosthetic leg, people find it difficult to fetch water, prepare food, and work. They become completely dependent on their families, who are already struggling in poverty. Exceed is a British charity that was created at the request of the Cambodian government, originally to help landmine survivors. Over more than thirty years, it has helped thousands of people in five Asian countries, including not only landmine survivors but also victims of automobile accidents and children who need braces and orthotic devices because of diseases such as polio and cerebral palsy. Having a prosthesis is the key to being able to work. Without one, people's arms are occupied with holding crutches. The big problem in the nations where Exceed works is not the cost of prostheses but the lack of trained professionals to make and fit them. Exceed arranges for people to study at schools of prosthetics and orthotics, but the vast number of patients and the small number of professionals is still a problem. 3D printing is one way of addressing the problem. It reduces the need to engage in a lengthy, cumbersome process.

Exceed has begun a trial using 3D-printed prostheses in Cambodia in partnership with Nia Technologies, a nonprofit Canadian organization. Using 3D printing will not replace the need for skilled professionals, but it could increase the efficiency of the professionals who

E-NABLING PROSTHETIC HAND DEVELOPMENT

To facilitate the development of 3D-printable prostheses and assistive devices, a group of people around the world created e-NABLE. This network shares information on 3D-printed prostheses. The group also curates a page for the US National Institutes of Health (NIH). The network supports the maker movement for mechanical hands by bringing together designers, engineers, physicians, 3D printing enthusiasts, and amputees and their families. The goal of the project is to create innovative hand prostheses by sharing ideas and 3D-printable designs on an open-source basis. Examples of the devices created can be viewed on the NIH e-NABLE website: https://3dprint.nih.gov/collections/prosthetics.

The e-NABLE project includes contributions from thousands of people around the world. For those who want to customize their own device, e-NABLE provides the Handomatic, which allows users to customize STL files with the proper dimensions for printing their own e-NABLE hand. A commercial prosthesis typically costs from $5,000 to $50,000. 3D-printed prostheses cost from fifty to a few hundred dollars. Because the designs are open source, they can be used by anyone, which will make a difference in the lives of people who would otherwise not be able to afford a prosthetic hand.

are available by making it faster and easier to produce prostheses. In addition to Asia, Nia is carrying out trials of its 3D printing technology in Tanzania and Uganda, in Africa, areas where prosthetists are scarce. Orthopedic technician Moses Kaweesa of the CoRSU hospital in Kisubi, Uganda, which is trying out the technology, says that it reduces the time to make a prosthesis from five days to barely two, and that it uses less material—thus reducing costs, which is important in a poor country.

The first person to test out a 3D-printed mobility device at the CoRSU hospital was a four-year-old girl who was born without a right foot. The birth defect kept her from walking and playing with other children. A prosthesis made it possible for her to run and play.

Nia's chief science officer, Matt Ratto, realizes that 3D-printed prostheses can work. However, he also recognizes the need to proceed with caution. In an article in the *Guardian*, he is quoted as saying, "We must be cautious. A lot of these technologies fail not for engineering reasons but because they are not designed for the developing world. You can't just smash in these new technologies." Nonetheless, 3D printing has great potential. Ratto's goal is to make 3D-printed prostheses for eight thousand people within five years.

The Future of Dentistry

3D printing is changing the way that many items used in dentistry are created, such as braces, dentures, retainers, crowns, and implants. In traditional dentistry, when dentures are needed, an impression is made of the patient's gums using a putty-like material. The mold is then sent to a dental lab that uses the impression of the gums to form the base of the denture, in which the teeth are then inserted. Often people have difficulty getting dentures that fit tightly or comfortably. 3D printing is beginning to be used in dentistry to streamline the process of making denture bases, reducing the time required to make dentures, reducing the cost, and providing a better fit. The process starts with making a scan of the patient's gums and uploading the data to a 3D printer, which then prints the base for the dentures. In addition to dentures, 3D printing can be used to make temporary dental bridges and crowns, bite splints,

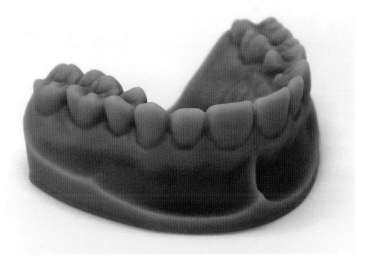

3D printing can create denture bases and molds, such as the one shown above, that fit better than those made using impressions.

and invisible aligners, which are worn over the teeth to realign them, much like braces. Many dentists still use traditional techniques when making such dental components, but the use of 3D printing is most likely going to continue to spread in the future.

3D Pharmaceuticals

There are a variety of ways that 3D printing could be used in the pharmaceutical industry, including customizing drug dosages, developing new delivery methods, and helping in research to perfect a new medication. 3D printing makes it possible to print prototypes of tablets quickly and inexpensively. So, for example, different forms of a sustained-release tablet could be created to study which version works best. As drug manufacturers start to see the advantages that 3D printing provides for making experimental versions of medications, they will most likely engage in more research and investment in this area in the future.

Currently, medications are made in standard doses, which often have to be adjusted for individual patients because people respond differently to an amount of medication according to their size, age, body weight, gender, ethnic background, genetic makeup, and the other medications they are taking. 3D printing could be used to create tablets in unique dosages, which is not possible with standard manufacturing because it relies on mechanically mass-producing large numbers of identical pills. Altering a manufacturing line to make a custom dosage would be prohibitively time consuming and expensive, but a 3D printer could easily be programmed to print a tablet in any dosage.

A doctor or pharmacist would be able to arrive at a suitable dosage of medication based on each patient's individual information—such as age, race, gender, and weight—and then rely on 3D printing to print as many pills as required. In addition, 3D printing could allow combination medications to be custom printed, for example a single pill that contains a patient's dosage of blood pressure and cholesterol-lowering medication, printed in layers. This type of approach could reduce the number of different pills a patient has to take, which could increase compliance with the doctor's instructions. The elderly, an increasingly large segment of the population, often have to take a large number of pills for different problems. For those who have difficulty remembering what to take when, having two or three "combination pills," composed of layers of medications, to be taken at specific times (such as morning or bedtime) would make it easier for them to take their medications appropriately. It is not possible to make such combinations with conventional manufacturing because each patient's combination of medications is different. However, with 3D printing, pharmacists could print such pills for each patient—and if a patient's regimen changes, it would be simple to make pills with a new combination.

Many medical experts believe that future medications will be customized to each patient to better treat diseases. Technologies such as genetic testing and new techniques for metabolic analysis are driving the field in this direction. However, current manufacturing techniques are not suitable for making customized medications. Shaban A. Khalid, Jonathan C. Burley, Morgan R. Alexander, and Clive J. Roberts of the University of Nottingham, England, are a group of researchers who have investigated using 3D printing to fabricate customized tablets in a size comparable to that of conventional pills, up to 500 milligrams (the size of a large multivitamin or calcium tablet).

On a desktop 3D printer that cost less than $1,000, they used a single-step 3D printing process to print viable sustained-release tablets in order to demonstrate that this approach could be used to produce customized medications. These could include multiple active ingredients, either blended together or in the form of a multilayered tablet. The team produced tablets that contained the active ingredient in the decongestant Mucinex. They were able to create printed tablets whose release of the active ingredient compared favorably to that of the commercial product. In addition, the printed tablets compared acceptably with the commercial tablets in their physical and mechanical properties, such as weight, hardness, and thickness, and their properties were within the acceptable range as defined by the international standards set forth in the United States Pharmacopeia.

Using 3D printing to make customized medication means that patients suffering from diseases that have a genetic component could have personalized medications manufactured specifically for their use, in the combinations most likely to work for them. The researchers also suggest that 3D printing could eliminate some problems with existing mass-produced medications. For example, nitroglycerin tablets are used by patients with certain heart problems when they experience chest pain. However, the tablets are known to degrade over time in storage, so it is not desirable to mass-produce them in large quantities and have them sit on pharmacy shelves. With 3D printing, the pills could be printed fresh, on an as-ordered basis.

3D printing has the potential to allow entirely new complex multilayer or multireservoir tablets, and other new forms in which medication can be delivered. The technology could provide better means to treat many chronic disorders such as asthma, arthritis, and diabetes.

TECHNICAL TERMS

cellular communication The ability of one cell to influence other cells.

reactionware A 3D-printed container with a chemical built in that reacts with substances that are added to the container.

synthesis The building of a more complex substance or compound from basic elements or simpler substances.

CHAPTER FOUR

Art and Science

3D PRINTING IS GOING TO ALTER APPROACHES TO BOTH THE arts and the sciences in the future. It is more than a technology for reproducing existing objects in a faster, less expensive process. The technology provides a means of combining basic materials into new and more complex forms, and doing so much faster than can be accomplished with traditional fabrication methods. This means that scientists, artists, architects, and musicians can create new forms not possible with conventional techniques.

Opposite: The flexible-legged robot designed by Mike Tolley maneuvers more easily than conventionally designed robots.

3D Printing and Science

Much has been written about the use of 3D printing in medical applications. However, that is not the only scientific discipline in which 3D printing is useful. 3D printing has the potential to create new materials in a number of other scientific disciplines, among them biology, chemistry, and ecology. The following sections describe some of the groundbreaking work that is being carried out in science using 3D printing.

Flexible Robots

The ability of 3D printing to produce components with complex shapes isn't lost on the robotics industry. Making robots that can move easily, especially over uneven surfaces, has long been a challenge. Researchers have difficulties with making robots that walk on legs, which tend to be unsteady, so today's robots usually run on treads, but these cannot always negotiate rough and uneven terrain. 3D printing could help solve that problem by making it possible to create new types of components for robots. A team of researchers at the University of California, San Diego, led by mechanical engineering professor Mike Tolley, has unveiled a soft robot with 3D-printed legs. The robot is made of soft components, giving it an ability to move more like a living animal. Its jointless, rubbery legs allow it to walk steadily across uneven terrain, including pebbles, and adjust to different types of surfaces. Professor Tolley notes that people have primarily made robots with legs that are bent in one direction, which are easy to mold but require a complicated design. 3D printing has allowed Tolley's team to create soft, hollow, inflatable legs. The researchers modeled the legs digitally to predict how they would behave on different types of terrain, such as a soft, sandy surface or rocks and pebbles.

The robot's four legs are positioned in an X, and it can walk, climb, and crawl, forward and backward, with a motion that resembles that of an animal. In addition, it can turn and move sideways without the need for sensors to evaluate the environment because of its ability to adjust to different terrains. According to Professor Tolley, moving one's body around in a very unpredictable environment is much easier when that body is soft. Robots that combine soft and stiff materials can adjust to irregularities in terrain that frequently cause today's rigid robots to stop. Robots with this type of mobility could someday be useful in a wide variety of applications, including search and rescue through rubble, and exploring tunnels and animal dens.

Modeling Cell Communication

Recently, Gabriel Villar of the University of Oxford, UK, and his colleagues reported obtaining 3D-printed tissues that enable them to create systems of cells that mimic **cellular communication**, which is the way that cells in the body communicate or influence each other. In some cases, cells signal adjacent cells by releasing chemicals called hormones. In others, a cell's shape changes. For example, this happens when a molecule of a medication in the bloodstream binds, or attaches, to a **receptor**, or port, in a cell's wall. Adjacent cells respond to the change in the first cell. This signaling between cells enables groups of cells to coordinate their activity, which allows them to respond as a group to changes in their environment. It's important for the cells that make up tissues in the body to act together. For example, if you flex your arm, you need all the cells in the muscles to act together to contract the muscle.

Villar and his colleagues used 3D printing to create networks of droplets in a membrane made of a biological material. The droplets communicate the way that cells in the body do. The droplet "cells" form networks that can be used in various applications. For example, they might be used to mimic living tissue for purposes of experimentation. The droplet networks mimic the reactions of cells in real tissue more closely than tissue made of artificial materials currently used. In addition, the droplets can be "programmed" to fold into specific shapes.

To accomplish this, Villar and his team started with a network consisting of two strips of droplets, and they treated each strip with a different concentration of salt. Over three hours, the strips of droplets folded into a network in the shape of a flower with four petals. Experiments such as this demonstrate that it might be feasible to use 3D printing to arrange living cells within natural or artificial structures made of biomaterial.

Saving Endangered Species

The poaching of endangered species is a major problem because of the belief that their body parts have medicinal qualities. As long as poachers can get large amounts of money for illegally killed animals, the animals will continue to be targets. The San Francisco biotech company Pembient is attempting to address this problem. They are working on a method of undercutting the demand for rhino horn, which is considered to have a variety of medicinal benefits in traditional Asian medicine. Rhinos are endangered, but they are extremely valuable on the black market. Pembient is creating 3D-printed replicas that are biologically the same as the real thing. The replicas are made with rhino DNA and the protein keratin, just like real horns, but they cost one-eighth the amount that poachers get for rhino horns. The company hopes to flood the market with the cheaper lab-made version, reducing the price people are willing to pay for rhino horns, thus making poaching rhinos less lucrative. If Pembient's strategy works, the same concept could be applied to parts of other animals that are highly sought after because of their alleged medical properties or their rarity, such as tigers and bears. The availability of inexpensive bioequivalent animal parts could help protect endangered species.

Conservation groups are skeptical. The International Rhino Foundation and Save the Rhino International oppose the synthetic horns because they don't decrease demand for real rhino horns and they add credence to the false idea that the horns have medicinal value.

Reactionware

Chemistry is another example of a field in which 3D printing is used. Lee Cronin of the University of Glasgow, UK, and his colleagues developed integrated reactionware for chemical **synthesis** and analysis by using 3D printing. A reagent is a chemical used to detect or measure a substance, or to convert one substance into another.

Reactionware is a custom container that has chemical reagents combined with the container material. The reactionware can be used to study how materials react with the chemical reagents and to perform various types of chemical analysis and synthesis. Synthesis is the combining of two chemicals to produce a new compound. Because reactionware allows reactions to be monitored in place, different reactionware architectures can be evaluated, and the most effective design for a specific type of process can be identified. In addition, reactionware architecture can be modified in a way that affects the results of a reaction. The chemist chooses the reaction he or she wants to study, then designs an appropriate reactor and prints it. The researcher performs the reaction and monitors it in place, using printed-in reagents for analysis. He or she can then alter the design and reagents, evaluate the reaction again, and make further changes until the product is optimized. Thus, 3D printing can provide a platform for discovering what happens with different combinations of chemicals and materials, evolving new types of products, and optimizing them, much faster than can be done with conventional chemistry.

Printing New Molecules

Someday it may be possible to make a substance we want by 3D printing its molecules. Molecules are the basic building blocks of matter. Each molecule is constructed of atoms, single units of basic elements. A recent article in the journal *Science* describes work by University of Illinois chemist Martin Burke. Burke has provided specifications for a 3D chemical printer that can be used to make thousands of different molecules, step by step, from a small number of starting chemicals.

The ability to build molecules from scratch would make it possible to recreate rare chemicals with desirable properties. For example, if a plant found in the Amazon has properties that could cure a disease but is very rare and hard to find, a researcher could theoretically identify the chemical in the plant responsible for its effect, replicate a molecule of it, make the chemical in quantity in the lab, study its properties, and possibly produce a medication with it.

The technique could also be used to print combinations of molecules that haven't been found in nature. Researchers could create and test combinations they think might have useful medical or industrial properties.

According to Burke, his machine could rapidly fabricate some molecules that would take a chemist years to make. He also suggests that someday his printer could be used by people who are not chemists to make molecules for new products.

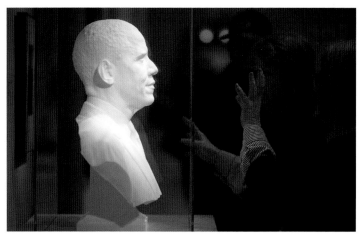

This 3D-printed bust of President Barack Obama was created for the National Portrait Gallery in Washington, DC.

Art

Among its presidential collection, the Smithsonian Institution in Washington, DC, now features a 3D-printed portrait of President Obama. The acceptance of the 3D-printed sculpture by a major museum illustrates how the additive art is gaining recognition. Indeed, all facets of the arts, including architecture, sculpture, photography, and even music, are being altered by the unique characteristics available with 3D printing, and that trend is likely to expand in the future. Artists are continuously discovering novel ways of using 3D printing and showing new types of creations to the public.

New Forms of Art

Numerous artists have become known for their work using 3D modeling, scanning, and other 3D technologies.

REPRINTING GREAT ART

People are captivated by Vincent van Gogh's painting of sunflowers. Rob and Nick Carter are apparently among them. They have used 3D printing to create *Replica of Vincent van Gogh's Sunflowers*, and they are not alone in their enthusiasm for replicating great art. Tim Zaman, a researcher in the Quantitative Imaging Group at Delft University of Technology in the Netherlands, is also an art lover. He has developed a 3D photographic scanning system to create 3D-printed versions of great works. One of Cosmo Wenman's goals is to digitally scan masterpieces from museums around the world and make the files available online so anyone with a 3D printer can produce 3D-printed versions of great art for display in the home or classroom. A number of his free scans of great works of art are available on his website: https://cosmowenman.wordpress.com. The replication of great works by 3D printing is likely to become a growing trend, given the ease of recreating the images. More than mere novelty, 3D scanning used in conjunction with 3D printing allows artists and students to reproduce exact replicas of sculptures for close study.

The following are a few examples of artists whose work has been pivotal in 3D-printed art. They illustrate the unique ways that 3D printing can be used in the creation of artistic works. To view their work, check out the URLs provided.

- Marco Mahler is a sculptor who specializes in mobiles, and Henry Segerman is a research fellow in the Department of Mathematics and Statistics at the University of Melbourne. In 2013, they created the first mobiles fabricated completely by 3D printing (http://www.marcomahler.com).

- Joshua Harker is a well-known American artist and pioneer in 3D-printed art. His work has been exhibited in galleries and museums around the world. Harker has presented his art through social media and the internet, gaining him international recognition and acclaim. His sculpture *Crania Anatomica Filigre* was the number-one funded sculpture project on the crowdfunding site Kickstarter as of 2015 (http://www.joshharker.com).

- Bathsheba Grossman is an artist from Santa Cruz, California. Grossman describes herself as an artist exploring the region between art and mathematics. She works primarily with 3D printing, creating metal-printed sculptures in bronze and stainless steel, often depicting intricate patterns or mathematical oddities. Grossman's works have been shown in art galleries worldwide as well as being featured in the television series *Numb3rs* and *Heroes*. In July 2012, her 78-inch- (2-meter-) high work *The Rygo* was installed in the VanDusen Botanical Garden in Vancouver. It was the largest piece of 3D-printed art installed in North America at the time it was erected (http://www.bathsheba.com).

- Theo Jansen is a Dutch artist. In 1990, he began building large wind-powered mechanisms out of PVC that are able to move on their own, known as Strandbeests. He has now created 3D-printed versions of these examples of artificial life, demonstrating the complex forms that 3D printing is capable of (http://www.strandbeest.com).

This Strandbeest, created by Theo Jansen, is designed to move by wind power.

- Gilles Azzaro, a French digital artist, describes himself as a voice sculptor. He set out to devise a system for materializing sound as if it were visible, using 3D printing to make sculptures of electronic **voiceprints,** electronically generated graphs of speech. In 2013, he exhibited *Next Industrial Revolution*, a voiceprint of President Barack Obama's 2013 State of the Union address (http://www.gillesazzaro.com).
- Designer Ji Lee started his Mysterabbit project in 2013. It is a street art project for which he has printed ten thousand tiny meditating bunny statues and hidden them in random spots around the world as tiny pieces of public art. He has secreted the small statues in locations from South Korea to Iceland to the United States (http://pleaseenjoy.com).
- Architects Michael Hansmeyer and Benjamin Dillenburger 3D printed *Digital Grotesque*, a 169-square-foot (16-square-meter), 10.5-foot- (3.2 m) high structure covered in intricate ornamentation. Their goal was to create a room whose architectural style defies classification (https://digital-grotesque.com).

3D Photography

It might seem counterintuitive that 3D printing is being used with photography, which has traditionally been a 2D medium. However, new ways to manipulate photographs using 3D printing are starting to be developed, and new applications will continue to arise in the future. A few of the areas being explored include the following.

Californian 3D printer company Pirate3D has started an initiative to make it possible for people who are blind to "see" photographs. The project, called "Touchable Memories," scans people's photographs and then uses a 3D printer to transform them into 3D versions. The final result can be either a raised relief—much like a bas relief, in which the objects and people look as if they are carved on a flat background—or a tableau of figures that are freestanding. Either way, people who are blind can "see" the images by touch.

Electronics giant Panasonic has recently installed a 3D scanning booth at the Panasonic Center in Osaka, Japan. Dusseldorf-based Doob-3D has set up eight similar booths in locations around the world. People can make a scan of themselves, and the company takes the data and makes a model, which is 3D printed to create a small statue—a 3D selfie. Creating a 3D selfie requires fifty-four digital cameras and lenses, a complicated 3D modeling system, and an industrial color 3D printer. Prices for the "doobs" from Doob-3D range from $95 to $695, depending on the size of the statue. One is inclined to wonder if the process will become trendy—in which case, competitors may enter the field, causing the price of these "3D selfies" to drop.

One of the hottest trends in parenting is prenatal bonding between a pregnant woman and her child. While many parents focus on ultrasound images, an Estonian company called Wolfprint 3D has created a service to provide expectant mothers with 3D-printed models of their unborn child, using ultrasound scans for the data to create the image. Mothers-to-be provide Wolfprint 3D with the files of the ultrasound scans, which are taken in hospitals to ensure that the baby is healthy, and Wolfprint 3D prints out the 3D version and mails it to the recipient. Wolfprint 3D is currently offering its service through partnerships with forty-seven hospitals and clinics in a number of European countries, including the UK, Spain, Denmark, and Norway. Many people find the concept creepy, but it has been enthusiastically received by pregnant woman, and the concept is likely to expand in the future.

Photographer Mathieu Stern has a YouTube channel on which he reviews inexpensive and unusual lenses. He recently undertook an experiment in which he used 3D printing to create a camera lens. Stern had no experience with 3D printing, so he made a prototype of a lens using glass from an 1890s lens and cardboard. Then, he used the measurements of his prototype to make a 2D design and sent the design to a contract 3D printing company to do the actual printing. When he got the 3D-printed lens, he used it to take photos, which came out surprisingly sharp. While his lens wasn't perfect, it demonstrated that printing 3D lenses is feasible, and it is a first step in a new form of lens design, which will no doubt see more experiments over time.

Cameras and lenses are made of a very complex set of interlocking components, and each piece must be manufactured to precise specifications. 3D printing offers the possibility of greatly reducing the number of individual pieces that must be assembled. In addition to reducing the complexity of manufacturing lenses and cameras, 3D printing might make it possible to create new forms of cameras and lenses. For NASA, using 3D-printed components means getting custom optical components faster and cheaper.

Architecture: Printing Buildings

3D printing is a natural application for creating architectural models that accurately demonstrate an architect's vision of proposed buildings and building complexes. Recently, architects and engineers have been asking the question "Could 3D printing be used to construct as well as design buildings?" Architecture and construction companies around the world are conducting research into using 3D printing to create buildings. Many experts in construction believe that 3D printing, sometimes referred to as "contour crafting," is the future of construction. The printing of buildings has a lot of potential advantages when compared to conventional construction methods, including lower cost, faster construction time, and less waste compared to conventional methods of building. It also requires less labor and material, further reducing the costs of construction.

Research teams have been experimenting with super-sized 3D printers that print building components. The printers use special concrete and composite mixtures as material. One of the advantages that architects see in this process is that it eliminates the need to build with mostly rectilinear forms. Because 3D printing can just as easily fabricate components with curved forms, the technology could be used to create buildings in a wide variety of shapes. The technology also lends itself to fabricating buildings quickly, which might be useful in areas devastated by natural disasters. It has even been suggested that it would be an excellent technique for fabricating structures in extraterrestrial locations such as the moon or other planets.

Experimental buildings have been built in a number of locations in recent years. In 2014, the Dutch design company DUS Architects started a project to build a small cabin called Canal House in Amsterdam, constructed of 3D-printed parts. The project was completed in 2016. Its goal was to demonstrate that printing a house on-site eliminates construction waste and reduces the cost of transporting materials. The parts of the house were printed using a 3D printer called KamerMaker (*kamer* means "room"). In this case, the parts were printed using a thermoplastic material.

Also in 2014, the Chinese company WinSun Decoration Design Engineering Co. developed a material similar to concrete that could be used in a 3D building printer. That year, it built its first house printed with 3D technology. The components of the house were printed on a printer 20 feet (6 m) high, 33 feet (10 m) wide, and 131 feet (40 m) long. The printer extrudes mortar in a diagonal crosshatched pattern with a hollow interior that acts as an insulation layer. The prefabricated components were printed in a factory and then moved to the building site and assembled. The house was then fitted with windows and doors. The roof was then installed, and finishing work was completed. The building cost about $4,800. In 2015, WinSun used the same technique to fabricate a five-story building.

In 2016, through a partnership between the government of Dubai and WinSun Global, Dubai set out to build the world's first 3D-printed office building. The 3D-printed building is over 2,000 square feet (186 sq m). It will be used as the temporary headquarters of Dubai's Museum of the Future. Although it will only be used temporarily, it will showcase 3D printing exhibition space and a small digital fabrication facility. The furniture and structural components will also be created by 3D printing.

Also in 2016, the Dutch construction company BAM Group and the Dutch architectural firm Universe Architecture produced a revolutionary new 3D construction printer. The printer, called the 3D Builder, is the first to offer a free-form printing technique. The printer accomplishes this by incorporating robotics used in the automotive industry. This printer not only allows free-form printing of structural building components but also allows users to create intricate ornamentation on the facades of buildings. The material used by the 3D Builder is a concrete aggregate consisting of sand and a binding agent. They combine to create a stonelike substance. The companies plan to enhance the printer's abilities in the future so that it can work with materials other than concrete, such as steel. The companies are also partnering with the Dutch robotics company AcoTech so that caterpillar treads can be added to the 3D Builder, allowing it to move **autonomously** on-site.

3D printing technology for construction is still in an early phase of development. However, there are great expectations for its future because it offers a number of advantages over conventional construction. New materials are being researched that could provide thermal insulation, transparence, and better strength, while being more environmentally friendly than traditional building materials. 3D printing technology allows architects to create buildings with complicated shapes, enabling the creation of more interesting buildings and the designing of buildings that are uniquely suited to their environments. 3D printing can create buildings that cost significantly less, which makes home ownership more affordable—potentially making it easier to provide adequate housing in low-income areas of developed nations and in developing nations. The major drawback may be a reduction in the number of construction jobs as the technology radically changes the nature of construction. It is likely that 3D printing will be used hand-in-hand with conventional construction in the short term, allowing more sophisticated buildings to be constructed. The hope of supporters of the technology is that eventually it will become a mainstream process that is used to build complete buildings from scratch.

Music

People have been experimenting with making 3D-printed musical instruments and are likely to continue to do so, using new materials and shapes. Some have made 3D-printed versions of conventional instruments, including drums, wind instruments, guitars, and violins. In some cases, these instruments are made of plastics or resin. In other cases, attempts have been made to mimic traditional materials and techniques. Many of these printed instruments sound surprisingly good.

One of the more ambitious projects was Harris Matzaridis's attempt to produce a 3D-printed violin modeled on a famous Stradivarius violin. When Matzaridis embarked on the ViolinoDigitale project, he combined traditional violin-making techniques with 3D printing. Matzaridis used as his model the 1677 Stradivarius "Sunrise" violin. In traditional violin making, various parts of the instrument are carved separately, and the violin is then assembled. Matzaridis took a similar approach. He 3D printed more than forty components on a customized RepRap 3D printer and then assembled them. Matzaridis printed the violin out of wood filaments. After the parts were printed, he dyed and polished them to create a classic violin look. He also carved intricate black designs into the violin, copying a process used by the famous violin maker Antonio Stradivari. After two years of work from conception to completion, Matzaridis's violin was ready to play in September 2016. It produces beautiful tones when played, and according to Matzaridis, the sound becomes sweeter with continued use, as with conventional violins.

Other makers of 3D-printed musical instruments have taken the opposite approach. Instead of reproducing existing types of musical instruments, they are making new forms of stringed or wind instruments, often in incredible shapes that resemble works of art.

Music technology researchers Joseph Malloch and Ian Hattwick of McGill University in Montreal, Canada, have taken instruments one step further. They have created a number of wearable 3D-printed musical instruments. They spent three years working with dancers, musicians, composers, and a choreographer to design the instruments, which are worn on the dancers' bodies. The instruments are lit from the inside and feature fluid, curved forms. The instruments produce music in response to the dancers' movement and touch, using advanced sensing technology to monitor the dancers' movements and transform the data into sound.

The architectural firm Monad Studio, based in Miami, Florida, has produced a quintet of futuristic but completely functional 3D-printed musical instruments. The five-piece set, called *Multi*, includes a violin; a small

The 3D-printed 3Dvarius electric violin is based on a model of an actual Stradivarius violin.

didgeridoo, a version of a long wind instrument played by the Aboriginal people of Australia; a single-string electric bass guitar, dubbed a "monobaribasitar"; a cello; and a hornucopian, a type of large didgeridoo. The centerpiece of the group is the violin, which is piezoelectric (producing electricity in response to pressure). Pressure applied to the two strings with a bow is transformed into an electric signal, which is amplified and converted into sound played through a speaker. The instruments are visually striking and produce sounds quite similar to those of their conventional relatives.

Clearly, the use of 3D printing has the capacity to transform art and science. The projects that can be realized with it are limited only by people's imagination.

TECHNICAL TERMS

intellectual property The inventions, literary and artistic works, or designs developed by an individual or company for which the creator is granted a patent or copyright guaranteeing the exclusive right to use the work for a specific period.

iterative product development The process of developing a product through repeated rounds of making a prototype and testing it, making an improved version, and repeating the process until an optimal version is achieved.

project management The process of planning, executing, monitoring, and completing work to achieve specific goals.

CHAPTER FIVE

Daily Life, Education, and Career

3D PRINTING HAS THE POTENTIAL TO AFFECT EVERY ASPECT of daily life: food, clothing, education, the home, and careers. This chapter examines the influence of 3D printing on all these areas. It discusses the future of 3D printers in the home and how this will affect the way that products are produced and distributed. Finally, it discusses the ways in which the technology can be used in educational settings to prepare students for the careers of the future.

Opposite: A student works with a 3D printer in her classroom. Such printers are becoming important educational tools.

Jewelry

Traditionally, designing and manufacturing jewelry have always required a high degree of skill in techniques such as mold making, casting, and forming metal. But affordable skilled labor is often hard to find in the jewelry field. 3D printing has the potential to create disruption in the jewelry field by eliminating many of the traditional steps involved in making jewelry. Companies such as EnvisionTech and Solidscape (a subsidiary of Stratasys) make 3D printers especially for the jewelry industry, which can be used to create fine jewelry using gold, silver, and gemstones. In addition to providing cost savings, 3D printing allows jewelers to create designs that would be difficult to form by hand, such as those with complicated and intricate shapes. Jewelers could theoretically make complete pieces of jewelry layer by layer using gold dust, but the cost of the material is so high that this is rarely done today. Instead, the technology is primarily used to create molds for casting fine jewelry.

Nervous System is a design studio that combines science, art, and technology. The studio uses computer simulation to generate designs based on processes and patterns found in nature. It then uses 3D printing to fabricate its unique art, jewelry, and housewares. Jeweler Eddie Bakhash, CEO of American Pearl, aims to use a combination of proprietary computer-aided design (CAD) software and a 3D printer to allow buyers to design their own pieces of jewelry, such as engagement rings, online. Bakhash is quoted in a *Forbes* magazine article as saying, "Now, with the advent of our platform, we're no longer taking off-the-shelf parts and welding. There's no jeweler at a bench with a blowtorch. The cost and labor savings is phenomenal. And we're empowering consumers to make jewelry in real-time." A buyer selects from a variety of options on the company's website, American Pearl's CAD/CAM software platform creates a digital file, and the company uses a 3D printer to create a model of the piece of jewelry in thermoplastic wax. Plaster is applied to the model to make a mold, and molten gold, silver, or platinum is poured into the mold, melting the wax and creating the piece in precious metal. The gemstones are then added by a jeweler. The process cuts down on labor to the point where the company can deliver a finished piece in a matter of days and at a lower cost than its competitors.

Even high-end jewelers such as Chanel are starting to use 3D printing in their workshops, primarily to produce complicated designs or to try out different versions of a design. However, they and other high-end jewelers fear that relying on 3D printing would diminish the cachet associated with handmade pieces. Purchasers who pay between thousands and millions of dollars for jewelry expect handcrafted work. Nonetheless, the use of 3D printing in the commercial jewelry industry is likely to expand. While most of the emphasis on jewelry making has been on fine jewelry made of precious metals and gemstones, 3D printing does seem like a natural fit for printing out complete pieces of costume jewelry–jewelry made of nonprecious metal in quirky and original designs–rapidly and in multiple units.

Fashion

The development of flexible materials that can be used with 3D printers has made it possible for people in the fashion industry to experiment with 3D-printed clothing. At a fashion show in 2015, fashion house Chanel showed a tweed jacket that was 3D printed, and other designers have shown dresses, capes, and gowns. 3D printing has been used to make fashion accessories such as sunglasses, hats, and handbags, but in the future, the fashion industry, which is known for experimentation and cutting-edge design, could greatly expand the production of clothing using 3D printing technology.

Initially, 3D printing is most likely to be used for custom clothing. Dutch fashion designer Iris van Herpen is the leading pioneer in this area. At fashion shows in Paris and Milan, she has shown a number of clothing collections featuring outfits that incorporated 3D-printed components. Her work is no doubt just the opening salvo in an industry famous for innovation.

3D printing can also be used to create unique combinations of fashion and technology. New York–based designers Xuedi Chen and Pedro Oliveira have combined these elements in a way only made possible by our

x.pose is a dress with a look that changes in response to data received about the wearer.

internet-connected world. The creators describe their dress, called *x.pose*, as "a wearable data-driven sculpture that changes opacity to expose a person's skin as a real-time reflection of the data that the wearer is producing." The dress consists of 3D-printed mesh over fabric. The mesh covers a layer of reactive displays, made of electrochromic film, that become more or less transparent according to how much information the wearer enters into her smartphone. The designers wanted the dress to reflect the nature of the internet-connected world, in which one's data is constantly being collected by online applications. Data is automatically collected via a connection to the wearer's smartphone in real time. The more data that is collected, the more transparent and exposed the wearer will become. An important aspect of Chen and Oliveira's work is that it illustrates the unique ways in which 3D printing, technology, and fashion can be integrated to create new approaches to clothing. It is extremely likely that in the future more designers will experiment with new forms of clothing using 3D printing, producing forms that we can't yet imagine.

Ray Kurzweil, director of engineering at Google, who develops machine intelligence, stated at the *New York Times'* 2016 Global Leaders' Collective conference that 3D printing "may radically change our relationship to shopping and our clothes," and do so a lot sooner than people think. He predicts that people will be using 3D printing to create their own custom clothing at home by 2020.

The major hurdle in the production of 3D-printed clothing is that the fabric that can be produced currently has a stiff, artificial quality because of the raw materials available for 3D printing. Kurzweil says this will start to change in as little as a decade. He predicts that a variety of new materials that are suitable for clothing and less expensive will be produced, and open-source designs for clothing will become widely available online. In this, he is probably correct, given that free and open-source designs have become available online for everything from earrings to prostheses. In addition, the availability of inexpensive 3D printers will make them a common appliance in people's homes. Kurzweil predicts that this will also happen by 2020.

Home-based 3D printing has the potential to put control of clothing design in the hands of individuals and small-scale entrepreneurs. This democratization of design could disrupt the control that major fashion brands exercise over the design and manufacturing of clothing. The combination of 3D printing technology and the internet provides easy access to both self-promotion (through venues such as YouTube and Facebook) and customers (via websites and online marketplaces such as eBay and Amazon). This means that anyone can design and sell fashion items, including both clothing and accessories. Just think of what has happened in the music industry, where individuals have become stars on YouTube and sell their music directly online. Although major brands will still have some marketing clout, the potential exists for new designers and new fashion trends to arise outside the traditional channels for fashion.

Food

Food technologists have applied every conceivable technology to the creation of food, and 3D printing is no exception. 3D printing of food began with chocolate sugar for the production of candy and cake decoration. Some other early experiments with food include the 3D printing of "meat" by building up layers of protein cells. Pasta is another food that is being experimented with. In 2017, MIT's Tangible Media Group used 3D printing to create flat pasta that folds into specific shapes when immersed in hot water. The group worked with a chef to establish the requirements for characteristics such as malleability and water absorbance that were necessary to create palatable pasta. They used a computer to create a prototype with the optimal characteristics. When they printed the pasta, they applied stripes of edible cellulose over the top layer to cause it to bend in hot water. The exercise was not as frivolous as it might seem. Making the pasta flat means that a large amount of space can be saved when it is packaged. The goal of the project was to illustrate how printing could be used to create new designs for food that were more economical. In addition to shaping pasta, they have developed forms that are colored and even transparent.

Someday, 3D-printed food may become a staple of both restaurant and home kitchens. Several companies are engaged in developing 3D printers for food. There are some 3D food printers, such as ChefJet and ChefJet Pro by 3D Systems, which work specifically with chocolate and sugar. However, the ideal machine would be one that can print a wide variety of foods. A major player in the field is Natural Machines, based in Barcelona, Spain, which is developing just such a general food printer, the "Foodini." The printer operates in much the same way as 3D printers for plastics, except that edible ingredients are placed into capsules so they can be extruded through the nozzles. It works the same way as a pastry bag except the design put down is controlled by a computer and not a chef. The Foodini can be used to create both sweet and savory foods, such as burgers and pizza. At this point, Natural Machines is designing Foodini to take over only the difficult and time-consuming parts of food preparation, which they believe discourage people from making meals from scratch. While currently the cook must puree or blend ingredients and insert them into the stainless steel capsules, the company is working on prepackaged plastic capsules that could be inserted into the Foodini, allowing users to make food without engaging in the prep.

The machine, which is about the size of a microwave oven, is particularly useful for making food that incorporates complex designs, such as decorations for cakes, and food with complicated recipes that require time-consuming, precise steps, such as filled pasta. The Foodini does not cook the food, but merely gets it to the oven-ready stage. However, Natural Machines plans to make a model in the future that will not only assemble the food but cook it as well. To give cooks ideas for dishes, the Foodini includes a touchscreen connected to a recipe site. Because it's a smart device, eventually users will be able to control it remotely via a smartphone. The company's website (https://www.naturalmachines.com) offers photos of a myriad of 3D-printed food products. Someday, it may be possible to program appliances like the Foodini to print and cook complete meals. Restaurant chefs interested in creating unusual and cutting-edge dishes are interested in the application of 3D printing technology to food, which they feel will give them complete control over food—in terms of both content and shape.

Using 3D printing to create food has a number of advantages. The technology could be used to provide nutritious food for people who live in areas where food is scare. For example, the gels to form the base of the food could be created from nutritious

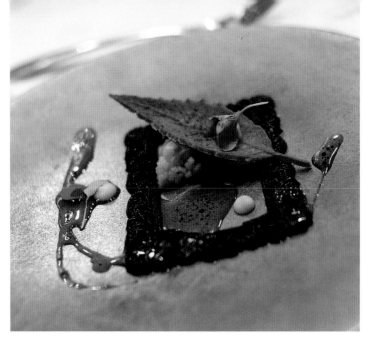

This example of 3D-printed food illustrates the intricate and fanciful designs that can be created.

substances such as microalgae, which contain protein, carbohydrates for energy, and antioxidants, while the finished product would be tasty and pleasant to eat. The Netherlands Organization for Applied Scientific Research has developed such a process for 3D printing using microalgae.

NASA, which is faced with the problem of how to preserve food on long space missions, is interested in how 3D printing could be applied to print food as needed from basic storable ingredients. NASA has awarded a $125,000 Small Business Innovation Research contract to Systems and Materials Research Corporation (SMRC) for the purpose of developing a 3D printing system to make food for astronauts.

Lynette Kucsma, cofounder of Natural Machines, suggests that 3D printers could make processed food more nutritious and palatable, for example by replacing fast-food beef patties—which are filled with preservatives because they have to be premade and stored—with ones that are freshly printed out. The technology can also be used to provide more palatable food to people who have difficulty eating because of age or disease. A group of retirement homes in Germany has started using 3D printing to reproduce hard-to-chew vegetables, such as carrots and broccoli, as soft, easy-to-chew molded forms that have the same shape as the hard version. Food could be made to contain specific amounts of nutrients and calories—or to not contain specific ingredients for those who have allergies. Italian 3D printing company WASP is attempting to develop a printer that can produce gluten-free foods.

3D Printing at Home

Manufacturers are experimenting with using 3D printing technology to produce everything from sporting goods to toys. The real triumph for 3D printing manufacturers will come when every household has its own 3D printer, used to print household items. In some ways, it is hard to imagine consumers printing out large numbers of household items—containers, toys, and other items they now run to Walmart for or order online from Amazon. At one time, it was hard to believe consumers would have any use for a computer in the home—much less in their pocket, in the form of a smartphone. Someday, desktop

3D printers might be as common as–well, 2D printers. The price of 3D printers will decrease, and their speed will increase. It's likely that, at some point, the materials that are used to produce products, especially plastics, will become available in a prepackaged cartridge form that can be inserted into the machine easily. They might eventually be used to print all types of household objects. Such a change will occur gradually, but it will likely occur–and once it does, it will disrupt the retail industry in much the same way that the internet and online shopping disrupted retail brick-and-mortar stores.

If people can print their own containers and bottles, they will be able to customize such containers to a size and shape that suits them. This may change the way consumer brands package their products. Many products may become essentially refills, sold in bulk to be stored in users' bottles and containers. Already there are open-source websites on which a community of users shares ideas and downloadable designs for 3D-printed products. This will expand exponentially as more and more households undertake their own 3D printing. At the same time, manufacturers are unlikely to let an opportunity for advertising go by. To promote their products, they will probably upload their own decorative packaging designs that consumers can download and print out on their printers.

The ability to 3D print objects at home also means that people will be able to make parts at home. This could change customer service for many types of objects

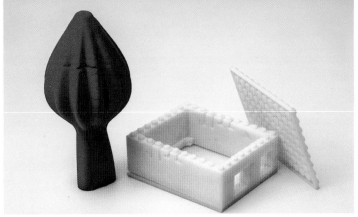

Common items like this 3D-printed lemon juicer and small box are easy for consumers to produce at home.

and devices. It might become common for companies to transmit a digital file for a part to a customer who needs a replacement part, and have the user print it out at home, rather than mailing the user a part. In the same way, companies could offer consumers the option of having different shells for smartphones or covers for a notebook computer. There's an obvious entry point here for third-party suppliers of designs for objects that can be downloaded and printed. For people who are do-it-yourselfers, products might be offered at lower prices without skins at all. An electronics company could sell the guts of a product, and people could print their own covers from thousands of designs available from the manufacturer or other sources online. If past history is any indication, consumers will combine parts in new ways and invent attachments to add additional features to commercial products. They will then either offer their products to others for a small fee, share them freely, or set up their own websites, providing the products for free but selling advertising, in much the same way that many websites operate today.

A bigger question is what happens when it becomes possible to print the contents of the bottles as well as the container. As mentioned, printers that 3D print food are being developed that rely on capsules into which basic ingredients are placed. Suppose it becomes possible to fill such cartridges (or buy them prefilled) with the basic ingredients to allow people to print their own cleaning and personal care products. This would create a market for suppliers of raw materials and prefilled cartridges while hurting traditional brands. It would also create a problem for companies trying to maintain control of their **intellectual property** and secret recipes. Even if the original manufacturer supplies the cartridges used to make the product, it's easier to protect a formula when one is supplying a finished product than when the components can be found everywhere. The widespread use of such 3D printing technology would change the nature of online retail because it would affect what people buy—fewer low-end finished products and more raw materials and cartridge sets. Certainly companies are going to have to adapt to the consumer changes that 3D printing represents, and technologies tend to advance more quickly than one expects.

Education

Using 3D printing in schools can help students learn better at all levels, from elementary school through college. In addition, using the technology teaches students valuable skills that will help them meet the demands of the jobs of the future.

3D Printing in Elementary and Middle School

Hod Lipson is a robotics engineer and director of Columbia University's Creative Machines Lab. He is the creator of Fab@Home, a multimaterial open-source 3D printer for use by consumers. Lipson, who would like to see a 3D printer in every school, demonstrated the Fab@Home 3D printer to his son's second-grade class. His project was simple—he demonstrated how to print a space shuttle from two colors of Play-Doh. The kids were thrilled and jumped in with ideas for modifications to the spaceship. To Lipson, this illustrated how successful the use of a 3D printer could be in getting children involved with math, engineering, and design.

Subsequently, the Fab@Home group joined with the University of Virginia to supply a few schools with 3D printers and age-appropriate software. Lipson emphasizes that 3D printing is a way to enrich the math and science curriculums in grade school. By engaging children in the practical application of math and science, Lipson hopes to keep them from simply deciding they're not good at math and science at a young age, and then trying to avoid those subjects.

Fablevision, the University of Virginia, and the Reynolds Center for Teaching, Learning, and Creativity are part of the Fab@School Consortium. The university and the Reynolds Center have developed the Fab@School

Maker Studio software tool. Fab@School Maker Studio is an easy-to-use web-based 3D printing/digital fabrication platform for students in grades three through eight. Using 3D printers in elementary and middle school encourages students' interest in STEAM (science, technology, engineering, arts, and mathematics). This type of orientation is important for their future. Today, jobs that don't involve technology in some form are scarce. Even the arts are increasingly incorporating technological tools. By the time today's students graduate, the use of technology in the workplace will be even more pronounced. Therefore, introducing children to technological processes and engaging their interest at a young age is important.

3D Printing in High School and College

As a student moves on to high school and college, 3D printing can continue to be part of STEAM-oriented education and learning. At this point, students should be capable of using computer-aided design (CAD) and digital modeling. As they develop an interest in a particular career path, they can use their knowledge of technology to pursue a particular area of interest. For older students, 3D printing provides a vehicle for illustrating concepts related to chemistry, physics, electronics, engineering, or art. As projects become more complex, students also learn design and **project management** skills, which will serve them well regardless of their ultimate career path.

3D printing could be used in two ways in high school. The first is to enhance the teaching of specific courses.

TRAINING STUDENTS IN 3D PRINTING

Countries around the world are interested in educating their children in science and engineering so that they can be competitive in the marketplace. Michael Gove, formerly the UK education secretary, announced a revised national curriculum for England's schools. One of the tenets of the new curriculum is exposure to and basic training in the use of advanced technologies such as robotics and 3D printing. To meet this requirement, UK schools will need to provide a 3D printer, software, and training for children starting in the primary grades.

This policy means that virtually all children in Great Britain will be familiar with the use of 3D printers, much as even young children are familiar with computers today. They will also understand the concepts behind designing and making objects. By they time they become adults, they will be well prepared to use 3D printing as a tool, which will make them and their country competitive in the creation of new products based on the technology. If the United States and Canada want to remain competitive in the new marketplaces that open up in response to 3D printing, they too will need to make training in the use of the technology an integral part of the educational experience.

In high school, subjects become more complicated, and 3D printing can produce objects that embody and clarify the concepts being taught. Examples of how 3D printing can be used in this way include the production of models of molecules in chemistry class, the structure of DNA in biology class, 3D topological maps or structures showing the strata in mountains in Earth science, and the recreation of an artifact in history class. The second way in which 3D printing can benefit high school students is by giving them the opportunity to use the technology themselves to create more advanced projects, providing an excellent opportunity to practice design and engineering skills.

In college, students should be able to undertake their own 3D printing projects. The following are just a few examples. Students who choose to pursue science or engineering careers could start inventing their own objects or products, using the technology to produce prototypes. Students can also use the technology to produce parts for experiments and projects. In fields such as architecture, the technology can be used to produce models and architectural components. It can be used in art to produce unique sculptural forms. In theater arts, it can be used to produce models of sets and props, and even figures representing actors, for use in working out the placement and movement of actors onstage. The use of 3D printing to produce practical objects gives the student valuable experience in project management and **iterative product development**–the process of developing a product through repeated rounds of prototyping and testing, making an improved version, and repeating the process until an optimal version is achieved. This knowledge will be useful when he or she embarks on a career in any discipline.

3D printer manufacturers are also leading initiatives to help get 3D printers into schools across the United States. 3D printer manufacturer 3D Systems has established the MAKE.DIGITAL Education Initiative to assist schools in obtaining 3D printers and related resources. 3D Systems is providing discounted classroom starter kits, downloadable curriculums, and training resources for teachers. Other manufacturers are also starting to offer discount programs, case studies, and training for teachers.

Careers in 3D Printing

3D printing is going to be a part of design and manufacturing in virtually every industry in the future. This development will create an enormous number of jobs specifically related to 3D printing. There will be a need for people in other fields, ranging from teaching to manufacturing, where some knowledge of the technology will be beneficial. The following are some of these future jobs.

All types of manufacturing and retail firms will require product designers, 3D CAD system operators, and 3D modelers, who can translate a concept for a product into a practical design that can be 3D printed. Some of the 3D designer jobs will be full-time positions. Others will provide opportunities for freelance work performed for various companies on a contract basis, or as an employee of a contract design firm that provides design services to companies.

Research and development scientists and engineers develop new products using 3D printing technology, such as a 3D-printed skateboard for a sporting goods company. They also develop new types of 3D printers and new materials for use with them. Medical and scientific researchers will work on 3D printing projects. From human cells to prostheses, scientists will be employed in the medical field to create tomorrow's health-care products. In other scientific fields, such as the chemical, energy, aerospace, and defense industries, people with 3D printing expertise will be needed to create the next generation of products. Research and development labs often require lab assistants familiar with 3D printing, as well as 3D CAD designers.

Blueprinting and model building in the architecture and construction industries will increasingly be done by 3D CAD and 3D printing rather than by the hand-construction of models. In addition, an ever-growing number of construction materials are going to be produced via 3D printing, which will require individuals who can operate large-format 3D printers. The construction industry will also require people who can design and construct buildings using such materials.

Teachers and professors who can train people at all levels—from elementary, middle, and high school to college—will be needed. Trainers who can teach existing manufacturing personnel how to use and maintain 3D printers will also be needed. 3D printing will produce new types of products and services. As 3D printing changes the nature of manufacturing and retailing, inevitably lawsuits and legal issues will arise. Creators of 3D products and processes will need lawyers well versed in 3D printing to assist them in protecting their intellectual property rights.

Whether a company is a dedicated 3D printing services company, a major manufacturer, a start-up company developing a new product, or a research facility, it will have a large demand for people who can operate 3D printers to produce both prototypes and finished products.

In the future, 3D printing will be a technology that is used in every part of people's lives. It will create products not yet imagined, disrupting the fields of manufacturing, retailing, and medicine. Being part of the future developments in 3D technology will be exciting, challenging, and rewarding.

GLOSSARY

adhesion The property of sticking to an object.

autonomously To be self-propelled and move without any guidance or control from outside.

bioprinter A type of 3D printer that uses living cells or the building blocks of cells, such as proteins.

carbon footprint The amount of carbon dioxide and other carbon compounds emitted due to the consumption of fossil fuels in the production of a product.

catheter A tube inserted into the body, usually used to drain fluids.

cellular communication The ability of one cell to communicate with or influence other cells.

composite A compound composed of two or more materials, such as plastic with glass fibers embedded in it.

computed tomography (CT) A three-dimensional image of a structure inside the body that is made by computer from a series of many X-ray images.

computer-aided design (CAD) A process in which a user draws a 2D or 3D design using computer software to create a "digital blueprint" of an object or structure.

continuous liquid interface production (CLIP) A 3D printing process in which a platform is submerged in a vat of resin, and light is used to harden sequential layers of the liquid.

cranial Having to do with the skull, or cranium.

elastomer Any of a number of stretchy substances that resemble rubber.

electrode A device that conducts electricity and is used to direct electricity through the nonmetallic part of a circuit.

electrolyte A nonmetallic substance that is dissolved in water to conduct electricity through a battery.

extrude To force, press, or push out.

filament A thread of material such as plastic.

fixture A piece of equipment that holds a part during the production process.

increment A small amount, usually one unit on a fixed scale.

intellectual property The inventions, literary and artistic works, or designs developed by an individual or company for which the creator is granted a patent or copyright guaranteeing the exclusive right to use the work for a specific period.

iterative product development The process of developing a product through repeated rounds of making a prototype and testing it, making an improved version, and repeating the process until an optimal version is achieved.

jig A device that holds a part and has guides for the tools that work on it.

low Earth orbit An orbit around Earth at an altitude between Earth's surface and 1,200 miles (2,000 kilometers).

magnetic resonance imaging (MRI) A type of medical scan that uses large magnetics and radio waves to make an image of the inside of the body.

micron A unit equal to one millionth of a meter.

nanometer One billionth of a meter; a human hair is 60,000–80,000 nanometers in width.

nanoparticle An extremely small particle, between 1 and 100 nanometers (1 and 100 billionths of a meter).

open source Available for use with no charge (usually with certain restrictions).

orthopedic A branch of medicine that corrects problems with bones and muscles.

photonic Using radiant energy such as light.

photopolymer A type of plastic that hardens when exposed to light.

polymer A plastic or resin.

project management The process of planning, executing, monitoring, and completing work to achieve specific goals.

propulsion A means of driving or pushing an object or vehicle forward.

prostheses Artificial limbs or external body parts, such as hands.

prototype A model of something from which other forms are copied or made.

quantum computing Using a computer that makes use of the states of subatomic particles (the particles that compose atoms) to encode information. A quantum computer has not yet been developed.

reactionware A container with a chemical built in that reacts with substances that are added to the container.

receptor An area of a cell that attaches to a particular molecule.

stent A springlike device inserted into a part of the body such as the windpipe or a blood vessel to hold it open.

stereolithography A 3D printing process that uses a computer-controlled laser to solidify a liquid polymer layer by layer to create an object. The polymer hardens when contacted by the laser light.

synthesis The building of a more complex substance or compound from basic elements or simpler substances.

thermoplastic A type of plastic that can be heated and shaped.

trachea The windpipe; it conducts air to the lungs.

ultraviolet (UV) A wavelength of light that is too short to be seen by the naked eye.

voiceprint An electronic representation of speech, showing the frequency, duration, and amplitude of the words being spoken.

FURTHER INFORMATION

Websites

Cyborg Beast

http://www.cyborgbeast.org

Learn about the mission of a group that is dedicated to making low-cost prostheses for underserved populations.

e-Nable

https://3dprint.nih.gov/collections/prosthetics

View a collection of 3D-printed projects, curated by e-NABLE for the National Institutes of Health, that have helped people live better lives.

Instructables.com

http://www.instructables.com

This site provides open-source instructions for making all sorts of things; typing "3D Printing" in the search box will bring up 3D printing projects.

MakerBot in Education

https://www.makerbot.com/education

This website offers a variety of 3D printing resources for both teachers and students, including projects.

NASA 3D Resources

https://nasa3d.arc.nasa.gov

Here NASA provides a growing collection of 3D printed models from inside NASA, which are free to download and use.

Stratasys 3D Printing Resource Guide

http://www.stratasys.com/landing/educators-resource-guide

3D printer company Stratasys provides lesson plans, projects, and other resources for use in the classroom at this site.

Thingiverse

https://www.thingiverse.com

A site for open-source designs that can be used for 3D printing projects.

3DHubs: What Is 3D Printing?

https://www.3dhubs.com/what-is-3d-printing

The definitive guide to 3D printing.

3DPrinting.com: What Is 3D Printing?

https://3dprinting.com/what-is-3d-printing

This offers a detailed introduction to the topic.

Videos

**BBC News: How Dutch Team Is
3D-Printing a Full-Sized House**

http://www.bbc.com/news/av/technology-27221199/
how-dutch-team-is-3d-printing-a-full-sized-house

This video shows how 3D printing can be used
in architecture.

CNN Explains 3D Printing

https://www.youtube.com/watch?v=e0rYO5YI7kA

The news channel provides an overview of 3D
printing technology.

**Digg: How 3D Printing Is Revolutionizing
Stop Motion Animation**

http://digg.com/video/3d-printing-stop-motion-laika

This videos explains how 3D printing is being used for
stop motion animation.

Lynda.com: 3D Printing Training and Tutorials

https://www.lynda.com/3D-Printing-
training-tutorials/6343-0.html

A variety of videos that teach the use of 3D printing are
offered here.

17 Incredible 3D Printed Objects

https://www.youtube.com/watch?v=FSu19nz7NlE&t=77s

A showcase of interesting projects created by 3D printing are presented.

3D Systems Video Gallery

https://www.3dsystems.com/video/gallery

3D printer company 3D Systems provides a variety of videos describing 3D projects and technology.

INDEX

Page numbers in **boldface** are illustrations. Entries in **boldface** are glossary terms.

ABOUT THE AUTHOR

Jeri Freedman has a BA from Harvard University. She worked in high technology companies for fifteen years. She is the author of numerous nonfiction books, including *Robots Through History*, *Career Building Through Skinning and Modding*, and *Spying, Surveillance, and Privacy in the 21st Century: When Companies Spy on You: Corporate Data Mining and Big Business*.